The Making of
HIGH-PERFORMANCE
ATHLETES

Discipline, Diversity, and Ethics

Debra Shogan

UNIVERSITY OF TORONTO PRESS
Toronto Buffalo London

© University of Toronto Press Incorporated 1999
Toronto Buffalo London
Printed in Canada

Reprinted 2001, 2004

ISBN 0-8020-4395-X (cloth)
ISBN 0-8020-8201-7 (paper)

'∞

Printed on acid-free paper

Canadian Cataloguing in Publication Data

Shogan, Debra A., 1951–
  The making of high-performance athletes : discipline, diversity, and ethics

  Includes bibliographical references and index.
  ISBN 0-8020-4395-X (bound)   ISBN 0-8020-8201-7 (pbk.)

  1. Sports – Psychological aspects.   2. Sports – Moral and ethical aspects.
  I. Title.

  GV706.4.S56 1999   796'.01   C98-931708-0

Chapter 3, pp. 48–50 and 68–74, is reprinted by permission from D. Shogan
(1998), 'Social Construction of Disability,' *Adapted Physical Activity Quarterly*
15 (3): 270–4.
Chapter 4, pp. 81–5, is reprinted by permission from D. Shogan (1991), 'Trusting Paternalism? Trust as a Condition for Paternalistic Decisions,' *Journal of
the Philosophy of Sport* 18 (1): 50–4.

University of Toronto Press acknowledges the support to its publishing
program of the Canada Council for the Arts and the Ontario Arts Council.

This book has been published with the help of a grant from the Humanities
and Social Sciences Federation of Canada, using funds provided by the Social
Sciences and Humanities Research Council of Canada.

University of Toronto Press acknowledges the financial support for its publishing activities of the Government of Canada through the Book Publishing
Industry Development Program (BPIDP).

THE MAKING OF HIGH-PERFORMANCE ATHLETES

Discipline, Diversity, and Ethics

Highly skilled athletes are produced by technologies of training that seek to create the athlete as a singular identity. Yet the disciplinary model of modern sport is consistently disrupted by the diversity and hybridity of the participants. Using Foucault's work on disciplinary power as a theoretical framework, Debra Shogan examines the effects of technologies of training and the ethical issues that emerge when demands to improve performance involve athletes, coaches, administrators, and sports scientists in decisions about how far to push the limits of performance. Making the case for a new, postmodern sports ethic, Shogan shows how the juxtaposition of hybrid athletes with the homogenizing technologies of sport discipline opens up spaces for questioning, refusing, and perhaps creating new ways of participating in sport.

DEBRA SHOGAN is a professor in the Faculty of Physical Education and Recreation, University of Alberta, and former coach of high-performance athletes.

For Gloria

Contents

Preface

My purpose in writing this book is to explore the complex production of high-performance athletes in modern sport. I am interested in looking at how highly skilled athletes are produced through technologies of training and how an array of ethical issues also emerges when demands to improve performance envelop athletes, coaches, administrators, and scientists in decisions about how far to push the limits of performance. I hope to show that what is ethically interesting about the demands of high-performance sport is not necessarily captured in the standard representation of participants caught in an either/or choice between meeting the demands of sport or following the rules.

What is of ethical interest to me are the possibilities available to athletes when they fail to meet the demands of high-performance sport. Fail they must because, despite the potentially homogenizing effect of technologies of high-performance sport, athletes come to sport as hybrids, reflecting diversity both within and among themselves. No athlete is only an athlete. Even the most dedicated athletes are members of families and communities; they likely have sexual lives; they are often students or employees. Athletes engage in discourses of popular culture, medicine, law, and citizenry, all of which inform and are informed by demands from disciplines of masculinity and femininity, sexuality, race, class, and ability. While high-performance sport at the millennium is still very much a product of modern power, the context in which high-performance athletes are produced is arguably a postmodern context, a context notable for proliferating and embracing diversity.

The hybridity and diversity of athletes make possible other ways to understand the relation of ethics to sport. Part of what I attempt to argue in this book is that the juxtaposition of hybrid athletes with the homogenizing and normalizing technologies of sport discipline opens up a space for postmodern interventions: questioning, refusing, and perhaps creating new ways of participating in sport. I see questioning, refusal, and creation as components of a new ethics for sport in contrast to an ethics that, in its present form, focuses on obligations to keep rules.

I happen to approve of high-performance sport in many of its manifestations. I do think, however, that there are occasions when it is appropriate to resist some of the demands that have become normal in high-performance sport. A new sport ethics that refuses normalization might make it possible to change those aspects of high-performance sport that are problematic while retaining and celebrating exquisite skill and experiences of competition that sport discipline makes possible.

There exists a large literature about the scientific, technical, and administrative technologies involved in the preparation of high-performance athletes for modern sport. I draw on some of this literature to understand how these technologies combine to produce 'the high-performance athlete.' Michel Foucault's work on the productive effects of modern power through discipline is central to this part of the project. By mapping the details of Foucault's account of the technologies of discipline onto sport, I expand and extend work introduced by others working in sport ethics and sport sociology who have taken up Foucault to understand sport.[1] This is detailed work that closely follows Foucault's own detailing of technologies of discipline outlined in *Discipline and Punish*.

If I was only to do a mapping of these technologies, I would give the impression that the homogenizing technologies of sport discipline do in fact homogenize and that athletes are unidimensional 'autotoms,' consumed by their sports. A significant portion of this work is meant to demonstrate the ways in which the diversity and hybridity of athletes make impossible homogenization and, consequently, the project of modern sport. It is my contention that a central role of a new, postmodern sport ethics must be the promotion and cultivation of diversity and hybridity.

My interest in this project reflects my own hybridity. I have had an unusual, one might say postmodern, career as a university employee. I was first hired at the University of Alberta as a high-performance coach and held the position of head coach of the women's basketball team for eleven years. After retiring from coaching, I completed my PhD in the Philosophy of Education; held a joint appointment with the Department of Physical Education and Sport Studies, and the Department of Leisure Studies, followed by a joint appointment with Physical Education and Sport Studies and Women's Studies. Ethics has been my focus in each of these areas.

It was while working in Women's Studies that I became acquainted with Foucault's work. My first attempt at thinking about Foucault's ideas was in relation to feminist writings that attempt to understand ethical issues for women in a context in which power is conceived as oppressive.[2] I was interested in understanding whether what counts as ethical and what is conceived as moral agency might be altered when power is seen not as oppressive or repressive but as productive of situations, problems, and possibilities. By taking up Foucault's work on disciplinary power and recognizing gender as a skilled, disciplined performance, it was possible to support efforts in feminist scholarship and activism that have attempted to undermine assumptions of 'victimology' or feminine passivity.

I have since returned full time to Sport and Leisure Studies and have had opportunities to explore the implications of disciplinary power in sport contexts with both graduate and undergraduate students. The ability of these students to critique high-performance sport while implicated in and in most cases valuing sport has helped me recognize that, while disciplinary power produces high-performance athletes, it does not consume their identities.

Many people have assisted me with resources in an array of disciplines from exercise physiology to biomechanics, and from coaching to sport for people with disabilities. I am grateful to colleagues Trix Baker, Gord Bell, Dayna Daniels, David Legg, John Hogg, Susan Shea, Trevor Slack, Billy Strean, Linda Thompson, Jane Watkinson, and Gary Wheeler. I would like to thank the following people for having an influential impact on some part of my athletic, intellectual, and personal life: Wendy Bedingfield, Lynn Bradbrooke, Howard Bradbrooke, Brenda Brown, Melody Burton, Laura Cabott, Lorraine Code, J.C. Couture, Marg Currie, Christine Dallaire, Dayna Daniels, Judy Davidson, Ivan DeFaveri, Sheila Dunphy, Elaine Filax, Gloria Filax, Maureen Ford, Pat Galasso, Joannie Halas, Lori Hanson, Pat Jackson, Pat Lawson, Sheryl McInnes, Gae Mackwood, Kathleen Martindale, Yvonne Mireau, Barry Mitchelson, Dennis

Nighswonger, Jean Noble, Robert Norris-Jones, Panda Basketball team members from 1974–85, Nasrin Rahimieh, Daphne Read, Faith Rostad, Sue Sherwin, Judy Shogan, Ron Shogan, Anna Smith, Malinda Smith, Angela Specht, Karen Wall, Jane Watkinson, Dave Whitson, Yoke-Sum Wong, and Earle Zeigler. Finally, I would like to thank Virgil Duff of the University of Toronto Press for encouraging me as this manuscript moved through the various stages of review. I am also grateful to John St James for his copy-editing skills.

In particular I want to thank my parents, Myrle and Lloyd Shogan, both of whom have a keen appreciation for skilled performances and who have lovingly encouraged my passion for both sport and intellectual pursuits.

A grant from the Social Sciences and Humanities Research Council made it possible for me to continue to work on this and another closely related project I am undertaking with colleague and friend Maureen Ford. I began writing *The Making of High-Performance Athletes* during the 1995–6 academic year while on a McCalla Professorship granted me by the University of Alberta. The McCalla made it possible for me to work at home, where I was kept on my toes by Ryan, who became a teenager during this time, and by a number of frolicking felines: bell, Bonnie, Drucilla, Elfin, Ollie, Orlando, Saffire, Silken, and Sekhmut. Thankfully, there was also the calming and intellectual influence of my partner, Gloria Filax. This book is dedicated to her.

THE MAKING OF HIGH-PERFORMANCE ATHLETES

CHAPTER ONE

Introduction

This book is about the making of high-performance athletes in modern sport and the ways in which diversity within and among athletes disrupts the potential for modern power to consume athletes' lives. Before I can address the disrupting effects of hybrid athletes on the relentless efficiency of sport discipline, it is important that I introduce what I mean by the phrase 'the making of high-performance athletes.' In the next chapter I detail the technologies that go into the production or 'making' of high-performance athletes and show that, through subjection to elaborate and minutely detailed organization of their movements, powerful athletes are made or produced. By powerful, I mean not only that an athlete is able to perform skills with strength and at great speed, but also that an athlete is able to produce skilled performance that makes it possible to act on others' actions. Production of actions as an indicator of power is implicit in the training of high-performance athletes.

In this introductory chapter I want to flesh out this notion of modern power as productive by turning to philosopher Michel Foucault. In order to do this I take up Nancy Fraser's assertion that Foucault understood power to be the same as constraints on action.[1] Understanding power as constraints on action and seeing that these constraints can either enable or inhibit action allows me to explore in more detail in the next chapter ways in which technologies of sport discipline are constraints that produce or 'make' athletic bodies that can perform the skills of sport.

Constraints are often thought to be restrictions imposed by someone who possesses more power and who uses these constraints to limit the actions of others who have less or no power. Foucault argued that power is never wholly limiting. In *Discipline and Punish: The Birth of the Prison* and *The History of Sexuality, Volume I* Foucault showed that constraints 'produce reality ... domains of objects and rituals of truth' including the individual and what can be known about the individual.[2] I want to say something more about power as constraints on action because, while many commentators and interpreters of Foucault adopt his notion of power as productive, few, other than Nancy Fraser, have made the links between productive power and constraints. In an evocative, almost throw-away comment, Fraser writes the following: 'Foucault claims that the functioning of discursive regimes essentially involves forms of social constraint. Such constraints and the manner of their application vary, of course, along with the regime ... Their obvious heterogeneity notwithstanding, all of these are instances of the ways in which *social constraints, or in Foucault's terms "power,"* circulates in and through the production of discourses in societies.'[3]

That constraints have productive or enabling effects resonates with me because of my understanding of the ways in which game rules constrain athletes' actions. Game rules enable certain actions and limit other actions by placing constraints on what athletes are allowed to do. Some of these constraints prohibit certain actions while others prescribe actions. Together these constraints on athletes' actions, produce what counts as the skills in a sport.

Because the notion of power as productive is not a common way to understand power and may, then, be difficult to grasp, in the section that follows I want to utilize what many already know about the productive effects of rules as constraints on athletes' actions to exemplify the relation of constraints and productive power. While game rules as constraints are merely the frame within which athletic skills are produced, what should become clear from using game rules to show the connection between productive power and constraints is that, when athletes embody constraints on their actions to produce or perform skills, they exercise power in their sport. Constraints produce skills and to perform these skills is to exercise power.

Constraints as Power: The Example of Rules of Sport

Like constraints that characterize or constitute other enterprises, rules of games *prescribe* certain actions, *proscribe* other actions, and *describe* boundaries or contexts within which these actions make sense. Prescriptive rules of the game of table tennis, for example, produce particular actions by specifying among other things what constitutes a serve and a volley – these constraints produce what is to count as skill in table tennis. Proscriptive rules circumscribe these skills by limiting what counts as a serve or a volley: hitting the net when serving, for example, does not count as a legitimate serve. What I call descriptive rules are a combination of prescriptive and proscriptive rules that circumscribe action by controlling space and time in stipulating the size, shape, and material of the table, the height of the net, and the size, shape, and material of the racquets and table-tennis ball. Action is circumscribed by the length of the table, height of the net, and texture and size of the ball. By constraining athletes' actions in these ways, prescriptive, proscriptive, and descriptive rules produce particular actions while ruling out others.[4]

There is no correspondence between prescriptive constraints and enablement nor is there a correspondence between proscriptive constraints and limitation. When the game of basketball was first played, for example, there were no court boundaries and hence no constraints on actions in relation to boundaries. Players spent considerable time chasing the ball in the gymnasium, which limited actions such as shooting, passing, and dribbling prescribed by the rules. Setting boundaries, encoding a proscriptive rule that stipulated that players must not cause the ball to go outside these boundaries, and indicating the penalty for doing so enabled participants to direct attention to actions like shooting the ball at the basket.

Proscriptive rules have been added to games over a period of time, not in order to afflict participants with ever more limitations on their actions (although this has been an effect) but to enable participants to perform prescribed actions. Accepting limitations on actions in order to enable others is not unique to games, of course. Drivers of automobiles accept limitations on their actions as they drive in order to enable them to arrive unscathed at desired destinations; musicians accept limitations on what notes they will play in order be able to play a musical score; academics rule out certain kinds of writing in order to make an academic text possible.

Proscriptive constraints, then, are both limiting and enabling of action. The extent to which action is limited depends on the number of constraints and just what actions are proscribed. Too few proscriptive constraints are likely to result in chaos while too many proscriptive constraints, though making it possible to pay attention to prescribed actions, create such rigidity that continued participation in the game or other endeavour may not be worthwhile. What actions are proscribed is also important. A single constraint that proscribes leaving one's home after 7:00 p.m. may be more limiting of action than ten traffic rules. Likewise, a few proscriptive game rules that severely limit movement are more limiting of action than a number of rules that prohibit movement in relation to boundary lines.

For each person in each activity or enterprise, there are an optimum number and kind of proscriptive constraints that enable the prescriptive skills of the endeavour to be attempted with some level of challenge. What this optimum is varies with the abilities or skills participants already have. Some will find certain proscriptive constraints more limiting of their action than will others. For example, a strong skater in ice hockey benefits from a proscription that limits holding an opponent in a race for the puck, whereas a weaker skater will be restricted. Activity is not enabled merely by removing proscriptive constraints, since some proscriptive constraints are necessary to enable performance of prescriptive skills. By limiting some actions, proscriptive constraints enable other actions, making it possible for athletes to act on others' actions and thereby exercise power.

Prescriptive constraints enable action by establishing the specifications of actions. If prescriptive constraints were removed from an activity, there would literally be nothing to do. But prescriptive constraints also limit action by circumscribing the range of actions possible. The prescriptive rules of basketball, for example, limit possible actions performed with the basketball to dribbling, passing, and shooting. Heading the ball, although not proscribed in basketball, is not an actual possibility for action as long as participants are serious about attempting to shoot the ball into the basket more times than the opponent.

Removing certain prescriptive constraints might enable some to act more skilfully in sports in which they are unskilled – removing, for example, the rule that prescribes 'spiking' in volleyball. It is also possible to enable some to act more skilfully by *adding* prescriptive constraints that correspond to skills some already have. For example, prescribing skills that require flexibility rather than strength may enable more women to act and, hence, exercise power.

Descriptive constraints can be enabling of action both by reducing chaos (which is an enabling effect of proscriptive constraints) and by creating certain actions (which is an enabling effect of prescriptive rules). By circumscribing contexts through, say, the use of boundary lines within which enterprises are to occur, descriptive constraints enable participants to concentrate on performing skilled actions prescribed by rules. The game of basketball as envisioned by James Naismith had no court boundary lines. Players played the ball wherever it went in the gymnasium, including the running track about most gymnasiums of the day. The addition of descriptive rules that set out the dimensions of the court eliminated the necessity of chasing the ball into these areas of the gymnasium, thus making it possible for participants to focus on attempting to shoot the basketball into the basket.

Descriptive constraints also set limits on the dimensions of an action or skill. The skill of shooting in basketball is framed by descriptive constraints that specify the height of the basket as ten feet from the floor instead of, say, five feet or twenty feet. The skills of soccer are framed by descriptive constraints that describe the ball as made of some resilient material and not, say, of wood.

Descriptive constraints enable certain actions by circumscribing the action to be performed in relation to a physical context. Batting in baseball is not just a matter of swinging a bat at a ball. Batting is swinging a bat of a certain size, shape, and weight at a ball of a certain size, shape, texture, and weight. Descriptive constraints can be limiting of action, however, by eliminating other movement possibilities (one kicks the ball at the net in soccer in the way one does and not in others because of the size and shape of the net). Removing or altering certain descriptive constraints may enable participation. Changing the field, goal, and ball size in children's soccer enables children to act and, through these actions, exercise power. In other instances, participants are enabled to exercise power when descriptive constraints are added – for example, the sport of wheelchair basketball enables action by those confined to wheelchairs.

What counts as skilled action in sport is circumscribed by game rules that frame the possibilities for athletes to act and therefore to exercise power. Being skilled requires still other constraints, however. The constraints that actually make or produce skilled actions are technologies[5] that make up the discipline of sport and that organize space, time, and modality of movement and seek to homogenize participants. These technologies constitute what Foucault referred to as disciplinary power.

Disciplinary Power

Foucault was a theorist of modernity. The focus of his work was on the emergence of modern institutions, such as asylums, prisons, hospitals, and schools, and on the forms of governance associated with them.[6] Foucault opened up dimensions of modernity not noticed by other thinkers, for example, by Marx who equated modernity with capitalism.[7] For Foucault, modernity signalled a shift to a modern form of power consisting of procedures, practices, and expert inquiries. By detailing these procedures, Foucault exposed the contingent and sociohistorical constructs of modern power and domination in relation to knowledge, rationality, social institutions, and subjectivity.

In *Discipline and Punish* Foucault traced how, within a period of eighty years between the seventeenth and eighteenth centuries, punishment changed from spectacular torture of a few lawbreakers, which made visible the power of the king, to humanist reform and then imprisonment and regulation of prisoners. The shift from public torture to incarceration with its technologies of normalization marked the beginnings of a modern, disciplinary society in which there was progressively less state tolerance for deviance and disorder.

As the scope of modern, disciplinary power was expanded and its tactics refined, new objects of discipline were taken on. Massive changes in demographics, economics, the law and politics, and science in Europe during this time required the production of large numbers of useful individuals. Mechanisms were required to control a growing and unsettled population, as well as contend with the emergence of a capitalist mode of production. Control over both the body of the individual and the social body was developed around two complementary poles: the disciplining of the individual body and the disciplining of the species body.[8] Together, these produced a supply of docile human bodies that could be 'subjected, used, transformed, and improved.'[9]

Modern or disciplinary power is 'possessed of highly specific procedural techniques ... [and] presupposes a tightly knit grid of material coercions rather than the physical existence of a sovereign.'[10] Discipline is an 'art of the human body' in which a 'mechanics of power' makes possible 'a hold over others' bodies, not only so that they may do what one wishes, but so they may operate as one wishes, with the techniques, the speed and the efficiency that one determines ... [D]iscipline produces subjected and practiced bodies, "docile bodies."'[11] That disciplinary power consists of 'highly specific procedural techniques' opens up the possibility of replacing the question 'Who exercises power' with questions about how disciplinary power is exercised. *"By what means is it exercised?" and "What happens when individuals exert (as they say) power over others?"'*[12]

The classificatory and controlling impulses of modernity are also found in modern sports, which emerged in England in the eighteenth and nineteenth centuries 'as highly rationalised representations of modernity.'[13] As I comment in the next chapter, the making of high-performance athletes is still quintessentially a modern project despite the fact that high-performance sport competitions now occur in a postmodern context or condition.

Foucault's description of a disciplined body as an effect of 'a meticulous observation of detail ... [involving] a whole set of techniques, a whole corpus of methods and knowledge, descriptions, plans and data'[14] could have been written about disciplined athletes in modern sport. The sections on 'Docile Bodies' and 'Correct Training' from *Discipline and Punish*, which itemize the components of modern power as it emerged in the eighteenth and nineteenth centuries, read like a 'how to' manual for coaches two hundred years later.

Foucault's work on disciplinary power, which includes detailed descriptions of how the organization and regulation of time, space, and movements train, shape, and impress bodies with the habituated gestures, procedures, and values of a discipline, has opened up ways for me to understand the disciplinary practices to which I was so committed as a high-performance coach. I am now able to spell out something I already knew – that those technologies that control or 'discipline' athletes in order to produce athletic skills also constitute the body of knowledge or 'discipline' of high-performance sport. Like other disciplines, 'sport discipline' entails both meanings of discipline – discipline as a body of knowledge and discipline as control, such that the body of knowledge that constitutes the 'discipline' of high-performance sport is knowledge of the technologies that 'discipline' or control athletic bodies. Disciplinary power is exercised both through the subject matter of a discipline conveyed through discourse and at the level of the body controlled through technology.[15]

The discipline of high-performance sport produces a set of knowledges about 'the athlete,' who is then controlled and shaped by these knowledges in a constant pressure to conform to a standard of high performance. Most advanced coaching texts describe details of how movement is produced, without, I dare say, the authors having read Foucault.[16] Yet, sport theorists and practitioners still construe power as a possession of some levelled against others – most often, coaches, athletic therapists, and administrators against athletes[17] – rather than as a network of practices, institutions, and technologies that produce the activities in which athletes, coaches, therapists, and administrators engage and that serve to sustain positions of the dominance of experts in sport discipline.

Utilization of this 'repressive analytic of power' to understand power in modern sport is modelled after prohibitions in law set out by a sovereign in which power is prohibiting, forbidding, and punishing. Coaches do, of course, exercise more power than athletes in most situations, but this power is not owned by coaches. Moreover, there are other effects of the exercise of power by coaches such as the production of athletic skill or perhaps even the resistance of athletes to what might be perceived as excessive interventions by discipline.

In order to take seriously disciplinary power as a way of understanding how power is exercised in sport, in the next chapter I detail how sport discipline utilizes technologies of docility, 'correct training,' panopticism, and the confessional to produce athletic skill and a set of knowledges about athletes. Foucault mapped essential technologies of discipline onto the army, the school, the hospital, and the workshop.[18] I map these technologies onto sport to show how sport discipline produces disciplined athletic bodies that are both subject to control and subjects of disciplinary power, the manifestation of which is exquisite skill.

Bodies of Knowledge: Power-Knowledge

An effect of the (prescriptive, proscriptive, and descriptive) social constraints of disciplinary power is the production of 'normalized' athletic bodies that are circumscribed by these constraints and hence both enabled and limited in their action. The constraints that control in order to produce athletic bodies are the same constraints that constitute the body of knowledge or 'discipline' of high-performance sport. As Marshall indicates, 'a body of knowledge is a system of social control to the extent that discipline (knowledge) makes discipline (control) possible and vice versa.'[19]

Understanding that disciplinary power is both an exercise of control and a subject matter makes it possible to understand what Foucault means when he refers to 'power-knowledge.' Connecting power to knowledge in this way is to indicate that 'power and knowledge directly imply one another ... [T]here is no power relation without the correlative constitution of a field of knowledge, nor any knowledge that does not presuppose and constitute at the same time power relations.'[20] 'Bodies of knowledge,' then, refers to the subject matter of the discipline as well as skilled, knowing human bodies.

As the subject matter of a discipline develops so do practices of controlling bodies. The practices or technologies of control are not, however, wholly limiting because they produce human bodies with skills and abilities. These are knowing bodies. Discourses of the discipline of high-performance sport provide the information that makes control of bodies possible. Through this control more knowledge is generated for coaches and scientists. This is knowledge about the athlete – observed, measured, and recorded by experts – but it is also knowledge embodied by athletes who can, then, exercise power through skill.

The subject matter or body of knowledge of a discipline is carried by discourse. Disciplinary power cannot be exercised without 'the production, accumulation, circulation and functioning of a discourse.'[21] There are two conditions that fix the limits of a discipline's discourse – one is internal to the discourse and the other is external. A system of rules internal and external to discourse governs 'what sort of *talk* ... (and which talkers) can, in a given period, be taken seriously.'[22] Within any discourse only certain statements are possible because they and not others are prescribed by the rules of the discourse: 'The fact that [a statement] belongs to a discursive formation and the laws that govern it are one and the same thing.'[23]

External conditions of a discourse might be thought of as external descriptive constraints. These constraints are the non-discursive contexts in which discourse is spoken, such as hospitals and asylums or professions and disciplines.[24] The meaning of a discourse or what is communicated differs with the kinds of contexts in which a discourse occurs and with the status of who is speaking and to whom a discourse is spoken. As Foucault wrote in *The Archaeology of Knowledge*, 'medical statements cannot come from anybody; their value, efficacy, even their therapeutic powers, and, generally speaking, their existence as medical statements cannot be dissociated from the statutorily defined person who has the right to make them, and to claim for them the power to overcome suffering and death.'[25] Statements by doctors within the discourse of medicine are taken seriously as knowledge, statements by patients are taken less seriously, and statements by homeopaths are not countenanced at all.

When legitimate speakers of a discourse communicate their knowledge and this knowledge is taken seriously by participants in the discourse, what they say is also understood to be true. In producing knowledge, power produces truth. '[T]ruth isn't outside power ... Truth is a thing of this world: it is produced by virtue of multiple forms of constraint.'[26] As Flax says, 'a discourse as a whole cannot be true or false because truth is always contextual and rule dependent ... Prior agreement on rules, not the compelling power of objective truth, makes conflict resolution possible.'[27]

'Truths' are internal to discourse. Attempts to adjudicate disagreements are possible neither by appealing to eternal, overarching Truth nor by appealing to processes of validation internal to the discourse to which one gives allegiance. This is because processes of validation internal to one discourse are often the very processes that are denied by a competing discourse.[28] Medical doctors are able to exercise more power in relation to health care than are homeopaths, and appeals are often made to the 'truths' of medicine to decide on the validity of homeopathy. That is, criteria of validation internal to medicine as a dominant discourse are applied to 'test' the truth value of a discourse with less currency.

For most of the next chapter I detail sport discipline as social control of athletes, but I also explore the discipline of high-performance sport as a subject matter or discourse producing 'truths' about the production of athletes. By virtue of their expertise, coaches and sport scientists control the discourse of high-performance sport and determine what is to count as a legitimate talk or truth about sport discipline. Discourse about high-performance sport not only produces what is to count as legitimate or knowledgeable statements about improvement of sport performance, the discourse enables coaches to be regarded as expert speakers of this knowledge and, thus, construes them as deserving of power.

Docile Bodies and Dupes

A disciplined athlete is able to perform prescribed skills with minimum error and maximum intensity in dynamic, often stressful circumstances. In order for discipline to create skilled performers, individuals must be subjected to detailed control of time, space, and modality of movement. Ignoring a training regime for even a short time virtually takes an athlete out of competition. Because high-performance sport requires conformity to technologies that produce skill and because these skills require repetitive, detailed training, and automatic performance, athletes may appear to be dupes controlled by a more powerful coach. Those who oppose high-performance sport often focus on temporal and spatial control of athletes, objecting that athletic discipline is indistinguishable from the training of soldiers in a military boot camp – a kind of rote, mindless, impersonal production over which an individual has little control.

There is a 'docility' involved in athletic training that is problematic, particularly when supported by institutions such as universities or governments that claim an educative purpose for sport. Yet, as Heikkala writes, 'sport is not forced labor; it must and does include a strong voluntary flavor. Significantly, the will to do better must also carry a strong internalized feeling of a "need" of discipline and conformity to the practices necessary for achieving the desired goal.'[29] Heikkala also reminds us that 'disciplines are not negative, they are positive ... the body is not passive, but active.'[30]

Foucault did use the phrase 'docile bodies' to describe bodies that are effects of techniques and strategies of disciplinary power, but 'docility' for Foucault was not passive. 'Docile bodies' are productive bodies – bodies that are able to carry out precise and often rarified skills. Nevertheless, there remains an ambiguity about using 'docility' to describe disciplined, skilled bodies. While disciplines produce performers who are superbly skilled, both the mechanical training to achieve skills and the automatic way in which skills are performed supports a concern that, while athletes are active with respect to movement, they are often passive in making decisions about the acquisition of movement skills and in reflecting on their continued involvement with technologies that produce these skills. Disciplines may be productive of bodies that can perform amazing skills but, during the acquisition and performance of skills, athletes seem to have little or no agency. Paradoxically, the dynamism of athletes on the playing field may be evidence of their conformity.

When athletes are characterized as dupes, it is not discipline that is criticized but the value of high-performance sport, since without discipline there would be no skills or abilities. Questions about the value of disciplinary technologies that produce high-performance athletes are questions about the value of high-performance sport and not a critique of discipline per se. After all, some of the most valued enterprises in this culture require subjection to an exacting discipline. Disciplinary technologies that produce skilled athletic performers are arguably not more controlling than, say, disciplinary technologies that produce skilled surgeons, skilled pianists, or skilled machinists. Like other constraints, the constraints that constitute sport discipline 'always carry the apparently contradictory forces of submission and empowerment' such that a disciplined athlete is someone 'who submits him or herself to the power of a particular way of knowing/behaving in order to participate in that power, to become more effective in applying it and thus to gain satisfaction and rewards that it offers.'[31]

Superb skills just are effects of exacting discipline. As John Fiske writes, there can be no argument against discipline in principle – 'no one would want to live in a totally undisciplined society, if such an oxymoron could actually exit. The conflicts, when they occur, are over the points of control where discipline is applied, not over the disciplinary system itself.'[32] When subjection to the disciplinary technologies of sport is criticized, the implication is that discipline is only appropriate when it produces 'worthwhile' activities and that sport is not a worthwhile activity.

The charge of 'dupe' could as easily be levelled at me as I write this book. Certainly the charge of 'docility,' if understood as passivity, is accurate since, while I am actively thinking, my body is inert except for my fingers as I use the keyboard. Moreover, sitting in front of a computer, spinning out this discourse, is itself the result of a range of disciplinary practices to which I have been subjected and that I embody. Am I a dupe under the control of this discipline as I produce the effects of academic discipline? To regard an athlete but not an academic as a dupe is merely to indicate that the effects of academic discipline are more valued than are the effects of athletic discipline.

Construing the disciplined academic body as an agent while dismissing the disciplined athletic body as a dupe exposes a Cartesian dualistic assumption about what contributes to knowing. On this view, academic discipline contributes to 'real' knowledge that can be stated in propositional statements: 'I know that x.' Production of athletic skills through sport discipline is thought to be inferior bodily know-how or procedural knowledge. 'Knowing how,' if recognized as a way of knowing at all, is not attributed the same value as a way of knowing as propositional knowing.[33] That those who produce technologies that discipline athletic bodies – the biomechanists, exercise physiologists, nutritionists, game strategists, sport psychologists – acquire propositional knowledge through bodily engagement with procedures and techniques in labs and other settings is ignored. This privileging of propositional over procedural knowledge makes it possible to contend that those subjected to disciplines that produce propositional knowledge are agents, while those subjected to disciplines that produce procedural, embodied knowledge are dupes.

Bodies of Knowledge: Athletic and Other Identities

There was not a year out of eleven years of coaching that the values and goals of the teams I coached were not compromised just as, of course, there was not a day in which the skills and strategies were not compromised. Compromised skills were almost always accidental, the result of an inadequate incorporation of skills and strategies and the impossibility of players making their skills and choices coincide in each instance with those of teammates in relation to opponents. Compromised team goals were also a result of inadequate incorporation of sport discipline, but there is more to it than this. Because even highly committed high-performance athletes have other interests, needs, and commitments, it is impossible for athletes to be fully committed to the demands of sport discipline.

While chapter 2 details how disciplinary technologies of sport discipline relentlessly homogenize athletes, making it possible for them to be identified or knowable as athletes to experts and to themselves, chapter 3 looks more closely at other identities an athlete brings to sport. These identities make it difficult for any athlete to be fully consumed by the demands of sport discipline. Women athletes, disabled athletes, athletes of colour, and/or lesbian and gay athletes have difficulty matching the requirements of athletic identity because other aspects of their identities often conflict with the demands of sport discipline. In order to understand how this is so, in chapter 3 I pay attention to technologies that constitute disciplines of gender, race, sexuality, and ability in order to make the case that, like other people, athletes are hybrids, the product of a number of diverse and often competing disciplines.

Sport Ethics: Conformity and Questioning

As a coach I thought it important not to have to check whether players were regularly doing their running programs, eating properly, getting enough sleep, and not drinking alcohol before games. It seemed to me that a 'good' athlete was one who was so committed to achieving outstanding performance that she would monitor her own behaviour. I had not yet read Foucault's account of the ways in which discipline succeeds through self-policing, but I believed that, if athletes agreed with the values and goals of the team, they would choose not to engage in activities that would be disruptive of these values and goals. I did not think about how to understand the implications of this conformity and I did not ask whether it is always 'good' for someone to be a 'good' athlete. What I realize now is that some of these disruptive behaviours occurred because of the impossibility that hybrid athletes could fully meet the demands of sport discipline. While I still think it important that athletes follow through on commitments to coaches and team-mates, I cannot agree with the unreflective conformity that was encouraged by my assumptions about committing to a team.

Not only does unquestioning commitment to a team and teamwork support the homogenizing technologies of sport discipline, a requirement that an athlete demonstrate that she is a 'good' athlete by conforming to an array of rules and standards assumes that it is possible for each athlete to commit in the same way. In chapter 4 I explore ways in which rhetoric about teams as 'community' or 'family' bonded together to achieve the goal of winning games is only able to be sustained by ignoring the diversity of athletes and hence the differential ways in which athletes are able to communicate, trust, and commit to teams. The imperative of teamwork requires that athletes and coaches trust each other even though coaches often exercise more power on teams than do athletes. Because relationships between coaches and athletes are often valued by coaches and athletes, I also address conditions in which it is possible for coaches and athletes to establish 'morally good trust'[34] between them.

As diverse, hybrid athletes are subjected to technologies of high-performance sport, a gap is created between the possibilities for homogenization and the limits imposed on this homogenization by the involvement of complex people. A reconceptualized sport ethics has a chance to have some impact on modern sport by working with and within these gaps to initiate what I call postmodern interventions. This new sport ethics stands in contrast to traditional sport ethics, which has focused on ethical issues produced by the demands of high-performance sport. In the final chapter, I take up Foucault's ethics of questioning, refusal, and creation of something new to argue for a new pedagogical role for sport ethics that encourages participants in high-performance sport to notice and question ways in which they are homogenized and normalized by sport discipline and ask how this implicates them in certain ethical issues. By questioning what is presumed to be 'universal, necessary, and obligatory,' the constraints of identity production in high-performance sport may become apparent to participants, thus opening the possibility of refusing at least some technologies of homogenization and creating other ways of understanding and participating in high-performance sport.

CHAPTER TWO

Production of 'The Athlete': Disciplinary Technologies of Sport

For participants in high-performance sport, discipline refers to an ability to stay on task and to execute skills correctly without being distracted. Success in high-performance sport requires and produces athletes who can persevere, who do not give in to competing desires, and who are strong-willed. To succumb to the pressures of a contest and revert to old habits of performance is a mark of an undisciplined team or individual and to resort to actions of retaliation or aggression leading to penalization, especially late in the game, reflects a disgraceful lack of discipline. Coaches and athletes understand that this discipline or bodily control under pressure is achieved by repetitive training and immersion in the drills that develop the skills of a sport. Discipline in sport requires control of athletes' bodies through the acquisition of skill and a sophisticated body of knowledge focused on how to produce skilled athletes.

Coaches realize that athletes become disciplined in the performance of skills as a consequence of 'a meticulous observation of detail'[1] in which coaches' knowledge about skill acquisition 'completely fills the time and space available with its required activity.'[2] Missing from coaching texts and manuals is a schema that details both how and with what effects sport discipline controls athletic bodies and the relation of training to the organization of space, time, and modality of movement.

In this chapter I utilize the map set out by Foucault in 'Docile Bodies' and 'Correct Training' from *Discipline and Punish* to schematize ways in which sport discipline gains 'holds upon ... movements, gestures, attitudes, rapidity.'[3] A project of schematization interests me for rhetorical reasons as well. I intend the somewhat relentless itemization of the detail of sport discipline that follows to be illustrative of the relentlessness of sport discipline itself. Those readers who are already familiar with Foucault's account of disciplinary technologies may wish to proceed to chapter 2

In *Discipline and Punish*, Foucault describes ways in which discipline proceeds according to individuation of private space; codification of 'correct' actions in relation to a strict timetable; routinization of activities according to a training schedule of increasing difficulty, followed by an examination to test abilities; and synchronization of individuals into a collective. Foucault mapped these technologies of discipline onto the army, the school, the hospital, and the workshop.[4] I map them onto sport and, in doing so, show how sport discipline utilizes these technologies to produce disciplined athletic bodies. These technologies are 'constraints on action' that, by circumscribing space, time, and modality of movement, produce skilled athletes who exercise power when performing these skills. As we shall see, the features of 'modern power' (what Foucault saw as the central feature of modernity) map very well onto sport, thus illustrating that the classificatory and controlling impulses of modern power are also central to high-performance sport.

Individuation of Space: 'The Art of Distributions'

> To a large extent, the sports landscape is made of straight lines, rectangles, right angles and semi-circles, all subjected to precise and accurate measurement. The geometrication of sport ... reflects the imposition of order on the landscape.[5]

In his important book *Landscapes of Modern Sport*, John Bale argues that the emergence of sports 'as highly rationalised representations of modernity' is reflected in 'their rule-bound, ordered, enclosed and predictably segmented forms of landscape.'[6] In this section, I show how this ordering of space contributes to the production of disciplined bodies.

The ordering of space was a central part of the change from premodern to modern institutions. According to Foucault, 'the organization of serial space was one of the great technical mutations of elementary education.'[7] From a traditional system of education in which each student worked with a teacher for a few minutes while the rest of the students were unattended and idle there was a transition to a modern education in which space was organized so that each student had his or her own place, making possible supervision of everyone and the engagement of everyone in work. This organization of space 'made the educational space function like a learning machine, but also as a machine for supervising, hierarchizing, rewarding.'[8]

The 'art of distributions' consists of technologies of enclosure, partitioning, function, and rank. Coaches must not only organize training spaces to create optimal possibilities for movement, they must understand both the ways in which boundary lines, target dimensions, and equipment constrain (limit and enable) the use of space and, consequently, how skills are, then, enabled and limited by these constraints. Defensive skills for defending against an advancing pass are different in basketball than they are in football because of the length of the playing field and are further circumscribed by the distance an offensive player is from the ball. Offensive skills are different in racquetball than in squash because of the shape of the racquet in each sport, the size and resiliency of the ball, and what is constituted as 'playable space.' Ceilings are inbounds in racquetball but out-of-bounds in squash.

The employment of particular defensive or offensive alignments in team sports can only be taken up in relation to the set boundaries of the playing field. For example, I wrote the following about the control of space as part of a defensive strategy to regain possession of the basketball: 'Let's see how the combination press works, beginning with a pass from a backcourt sideline. We start in an aggressive [player-to-player defence], contesting the inbounds pass. If the inbounds pass is completed, the defender on the ball plays aggressively, attempting to force the dribbler toward the sideline at midcourt.'[9]

The organization of this midcourt press is only possible in relation to the spatial constraints of the basketball court – sidelines, end lines, midcourt lines. To manipulate space strategically during competition, space must be organized during practice sessions in order that athletes always know where they are in relation to opponents, team-mates, implements, targets, and boundaries. In order for athletes to acquire a bodily understanding of where they are, coaches must eliminate distractions by ensuring, whenever possible, that practice space is separated from those not engaged in the training session. For discipline to do its work, it is important to *enclose* space and in so doing specify it as different from other space to 'derive the maximum advantages and to neutralize the inconveniences.'[10] As a coach, I was concerned that no one but the team and assistants were in the gymnasium during practice sessions in order to eliminate distractions caused by people walking through the gymnasium and to protect equipment from possible theft. Having a separate space to practice served to designate the space as belonging to this team and to reinforce players' sense of the seriousness of the session.

The team was enclosed within a space that contained three cross-court basketball courts and one full basketball court with a total of eight basketball hoops. Practice sessions were organized in relation to all or some of these four courts. Players were often subdivided into smaller groups at these stations. Subdivision into smaller groups prevented idleness and made it possible for me to ensure that everyone was engaged in the assigned task. A frequently used drill began with the instruction 'confined space.' At this verbal cue, players paired up and practised a ball handling–defensive footwork drill within the length of a court but confined by marked spots on the floor about ten feet apart, not overlapping the space of other players. By confining athletes' movements to this space, I was able to see everyone practising skills often required in games – dribbling while closely guarded within a space in which there was no room to break away or defending against someone attempting to advance the ball up the floor.

Partitioning eliminates 'the uncontrolled disappearance of individuals, their diffuse circulation, their unusable and dangerous coagulation.'[11] While these concerns are less likely in a practice session of high-performance athletes, they are often a concern in instructional sessions in schools, for example, where it is possible for individuals to slip out of teaching sessions when congregated in large groups, or for any discontent with the instructor to grow in the large group. The advantages of partitioning, as Foucault describes it, are that it aims to 'establish presences and absences, to know where and how to locate individuals, to set up useful communications, to interrupt others, to be able at each moment to supervise the conduct of each individual, to assess it, judge it, calculate its qualities or merits. It was a procedure, therefore, aimed at knowing, mastering and using.'[12]

Partitioning of players into spaces within the larger enclosure 'eliminate[s] the effects of imprecise distributions.'[13] Instances are avoided in which athletes watch some few others perform. As well, movements that are extraneous to the skill are eliminated. When practising shooting, athletes are stationed close to baskets, thus eliminating the necessity of moving to the basket in order to shoot or shooting from a distance that would not likely occur in a competition.

Enclosures within the larger enclosure are *functional sites*. They create a useful space.[14] If skill acquisition is to have any function in a competition, organization of space during practice sessions must replicate competition as much as possible. Each player is partitioned on the floor according to his or her function on the team or according to a particular sequence of possibilities. Although the distribution of players on a basketball court is not as predictable, say, as that of students in a classroom or workers in a workplace, there are limits on where a player may go and these limits are related to their function within the space. In football, for example, each player assumes an assigned position in relation to team-mates and relevant to the function to be served in the next play sequence. That there are certain skills that can only be performed when players are situated in particular places on the court is apparent from the following: 'As the ball approaches midcourt area, we apply a double-team, preferably with two frontline players ... If that's not possible, the double-team may be initiated by the back line player nearest the ball ... As the second defender begins to double up on the dribbler at midcourt, the other defenders immediately go into the 2-2-1 zone.'[15]

Partitioning players in practices and competitions makes it possible for a coach to make an assessment of the differences in skill acquisition among players that enables further partitioning of players according to their level of skill. Distribution of players into designated spaces for skill acquisition allows coaches to *rank*[16] players. For example, in a weight-training room, the particular exercise sites remain fixed and athletes move as they acquire skill or need remedial work on a skill. Coaches have in their heads, or at least on paper, a series of grids and charts with information about what activities athletes are capable of performing. They have at their disposal what Foucault called *tableaux vivants* – living tables – that provides a means to both organize and control the activities to be performed by any individual when they occupy a particular space or role. As Foucault indicated, 'supervision and intelligibility ... are inextricably bound up.'[17]

The technologies that make up 'the art of distribution' – enclosure, partitioning, function, and rank – have the effect of demarcating athletes architecturally, functionally, and hierarchically.[18] Architectural enclosures make it possible for athletes to learn and use skills continuously and without interruption. Enclosures also serve to reinforce hierarchal boundaries between who is to count as an athlete and who is not and which athletes are more important than other athletes. When I first began coaching in the early 1970s, the enclosure that marked off the main gymnasium also marked off the space reserved for the men's basketball team. The women's basketball team and the men's and women's volleyball teams did not practise within that enclosure, even though their home competitions were scheduled there. The enclosure in which each team practised marked its relative importance in the hierarchy of teams on campus at that time. The architectural enclosure of the main gymnasium served to consolidate the boundary between athletes and non-athletes and between 'real' athletes and 'pseudo' athletes.[19]

Embodied Time: 'Control of Activity'

Descriptive constraints establish the spatial limitations and possibilities that circumscribe skills and they establish temporal limits and possibilities for skills; these temporal limits are often codified in relation to spatial constraints. In basketball there is a specified amount of time for the contest; there are temporal constraints in relation to the time to advance the basketball from the backcourt to the frontcourt; time to shoot the basketball at the basket once in possession of the ball; time to inbounds the ball or shoot the ball during a foul shot; and time spent in the key area in front of the basket.

There are other temporal constraints not codified in rule books but taken up by coaches to manipulate the limitations and possibilities presented by codified time constraints. These include manipulations of tempo. The embodiment of a tempo at which skills are to be performed and the tempo of team manoeuvres is affected by the intensity in practice sessions of repetitions. Tempo in a game like basketball can be affected in the transition from offence to defence (by putting pressure on the player with the basketball) and from defence to offence (by an organized movement of the basketball up the floor).

Understanding the spatial constraints of an activity is necessary if players are to become disciplined in their movements, but this discipline will remain discrete with no relation to other activities unless it is possible to specify how activities should be coordinated.[20] Activities are coordinated by 'timetables,' 'temporal elaboration of the act,' 'correlation of the body and the gesture,' 'body-object articulation,' and 'exhaustive use.'

The Timetable

'8.45 entrance of the monitor, 8.52 the monitor's summons, 8.56 entrance of the children and prayer, 9.00 the children go to their benches, 9.04 first slate, 9.08 end of dictation, 9.12 second slate, etc.'[21]

The minute organization of time practised in elementary schools in the early nineteenth century may not be as prevalent in schools in the latter part of the twentieth century, but it is still very prevalent in high-performance sport. For one thing, coaches are intolerant of those who arrive late at practice. 'When [players show up late for practice], the best way to handle it is to have a standard rule that players arriving late go ahead and dress out, do stretching or limbering up exercises on the sidelines until the next shooting drill or water break, and then report to the head coach to discuss the reason for their tardiness. If their excuse is valid, they can join practice; if not, they are dismissed for the day (and possibly the next day as well). But in all cases the problem should be dealt with quickly, quietly, and forcefully.'[22]

In basketball practice sessions, it is common not to spend more than five or ten minutes on a drill, with very little transition time from drill to drill. Many coaches use the game clock to indicate the time for each drill and run the clock during the drill so that everyone can see how much time is remaining. When the buzzer sounds, players move to the next drill and the manager puts up the next designated time. The sequence of drills and the time for each are preplanned according to a timetable that designates how each minute of the practice is to be spent (see table 2.1).

'Precision and application are, with regularity, the fundamental virtues of disciplinary time.'[23] The timetable makes it possible for coaches to rule out unnecessary actions and concentrate effort on activities designed to improve skill. Preparing high-performance athletes requires 'totally use-

TABLE 2.1 University of Alberta, Panda Basketball practice session,
24 January 1985

5:00–5:10	full-court lay-up drill
5:10–5:15	defensive drill: confined space
5:15–5:20	blocking out: emphasize non-ballside block out
5:20–5:30	timed shooting drill
5:30–5:40	fast break drill with pressure points
5:40–5:50	defence against double post offence
5:50–6:00	3 on 2 conditioner
6:00–6:10	half-court press
6:10–6:15	shooting with pressure
6:15–6:25	offense vs. 2-1-2 zone
6:25–6:35	strategic situations
6:35–6:45	scrimmage, alternating zone with player-player; full-court with half-court press
6:45–6:55	lines – timed
6:55–7:00	free-throw shooting

ful time ... a time of good quality, throughout which the body is constantly applied to its exercise.'[24] As the Theory II manual of the National Coaching Certification Program indicates: 'It takes *time* to learn. It also takes spending the *appropriate amount of time on the appropriate task* ... But spending time on appropriate tasks is not enough – skill development *means* having a high success rate on a key skill over a meaningful period of time.'[25]

In order to ensure efficient use of time, coaches must be masters of the timetable. A coach must not only have time organized for daily practices, he or she must have a timetable to establish a rhythmic training schedule that follows the 'seasons' – the postseason and preseason – and time scheduled for conditioning, psychological preparation, skill development, teamwork, and strategy. Without timetables, coaches would be unable to establish training cycles or the rhythms of specific activities. Nor would they be able to regulate cycles of repetition.[26] *Repetition* of skills under competition conditions is central to disciplined performance.

The Temporal Elaboration of the Act

> The length of the short step will be a foot, that of the ordinary step, the double step and the marching step will be two feet, the whole measured from one heel to the next; as for the duration, that of the ordinary step and the marching step will last one second, during which two double steps would be performed; the duration of the marching step will be a little longer than one second.[27]

The lay-up shot in basketball is one of many skills that requires coordination of the components of the skill as well as a direction, a sequential order, and a duration for each of the movements.[28] The lay-up shot consists of one and a half steps while carrying the ball. The first step is a half-step because it is performed while picking up the ball from a dribble or pass, yet it is the longer of the 'two' steps both in distance and in duration because it moves the player horizontally while the second step takes the player vertically toward the basket. The lay-up shot involves a rhythm – a temporal sequencing – the elaboration of which a player must incorporate if the shot is to be performed correctly. Time must penetrate the body.[29]

To assist a player in acquiring the rhythm for the lay-up, footwork is usually learned first – 'one, two-up; one, two-up; one, two-up' over and over with the emphasis on an elongated first step and short, propulsive second step. '[There is a] precision in the breakdown of gestures and movements, another way of adjusting the body to temporal imperatives.'[30] While there is considerable room for variation in the lay-up shot, primarily in relation to timing the release of the ball, this shot would not be the same shot, and would probably be proscribed by the rules, if the first step was vertical and the second was horizontal and/or if the first step was very short in duration in relation to a very-long-in-duration second step.

Correlation of the Body and the Gesture

> Good handwriting ... presupposes a gymnastics – a whole routine whose rigorous code invests the body in its entirety, from the points of the feet to the tip of the index finger.[31]

The player's feet are shoulder width apart, back is straight, knees and hips bent at about a forty-five-degree angle. The shot is begun by placing the shooting hand directly under the ball with the nonshooting hand as support. The force required to shoot the ball is a summation of the forces, which are generated sequentially by extending first the ankles, followed by the knees, hips, and elbows. The accumulated force is directed through the centre of the body and up and through the basketball which is sitting on the palm of the shooting hand. The ball is released by flexing the wrist of the shooting hand. The nonshooting hand opens to come off the ball with the arm remaining above the shoulder.[32]

When I learned to shoot a basketball, instructional techniques were minimal: aim at the basket, use your legs, shoot with one hand using the nondominant hand as a guide. It is little wonder that I was never a very accurate shooter from any distance. One of the reasons why I was not a very accurate shooter was that I was unaware that I needed to correlate what the rest of my body was doing with my arm that shot the ball. I became a better shooter when I started coaching and became intent upon identifying what every part of the body was to do when shooting the basketball.

Time is only used correctly if movement is efficient – if 'everything is called upon to form the support of the act required.'[33] Shooting a basketball is not merely a matter of performing a 'series of particular gestures.' If one is to be a disciplined shooter, one must achieve 'the best relation between a gesture and the overall position of the body, which is its condition of efficiency and speed. In the correct use of the body, which makes possible a correct use of time, nothing must remain idle or useless: everything must be called upon to form the support of the act required.'[34] Good shooters and good coaches of good shooters know that if the feet, ankles, knees, hips, head, and eyes are not supporting the shoulders, arms, wrist, and hands, any ball that goes through the basketball hoop arrived there accidentally.

The Body-Object Articulation

Bring the weapon forward. In three stages. Raise the rifle with the right hand, bringing it close to the body so as to hold it perpendicular with the

right knee, the end of the barrel at eye level ... At the second stage, bring
the rifle in front of you with the left hand, the barrel in the middle between
the two eyes ... At the third stage, let go of the rifle with the left hand, which
falls along the thigh, raising the rifle with the right hand, the lock outwards
and opposite the chest.[35]

Most high-performance sport involves the articulation of the body
with one or more objects or implements. Baseball players articulate with
the baseball, their gloves, and the bat; rowers with their boats and oars;
synchronized swimmers with the water and their props; even distance
runners must articulate with the track. Some sports require a more
sophisticated breakdown of the movements of a skill in relation to the
object. While basketball players need only concern themselves with one
object to manipulate, there are a number of skills involving articulation
with the basketball. These include variations on shooting, dribbling, passing, and blocking.

For a player to become disciplined in relation to the basketball to be
manipulated, 'the total gesture' is broken down into 'two parallel series':
the parts of the body to be used and the object to be manipulated. Once
each of these is mastered, they are 'correlated together according to a
number of simple gestures' and in a 'canonical succession in which each
of these correlations occupies a particular place.'[36] The reverse dribble is
a skill that is performed in specific circumstances, when attempting to
change direction when closely defended. The reverse dribble consists of a
particular type of footwork while manipulating the basketball. In order to
acquire this skill, players must master the footwork and ball-handling
techniques before putting the two together as described below:

Reverse footwork: The player plants the foot to the side she wishes to reverse
direction. The knee bends and the centre of gravity drops. The arm opposite the side of the planted foot is swung back to help rotate the body backward. The stepping foot remains close to the floor and the weight shifts
between pivot foot and the stepping foot in order to maintain balance.
Reverse dribble: While the player plants her foot, she keeps the elbow of her
dribbling arm close to her body to ensure that the force is directed through
the centre of the ball. As the player pivots backward, the ball is bounced
once between her feet and close to her body. After this single dribble, the

player contacts the ball with her opposite hand, as she steps in the new direction.'[37]

Like the lay-up shot, the reverse dribble is best learned by isolating the footwork from the movement of the ball. Not mentioned in the instructions above is a sequence isolating ball movement from footwork that must be embodied before footwork and ball movements are combined in the reverse dribble. Players embody an understanding of the circumstances in which a reverse dribble is performed by attempting to advance the ball through a dribble while closely defended. The 'confined space' drill I described earlier helps correlate movements in a prescribed succession.

Foucault writes that 'over the whole surface of contact between the body and the object it handles, power is introduced, fastening them to one another.'[38] The articulation of bodies and objects is a technological constraint that enables skilled athletes, in this case basketball players, to perform a range of manipulations of the basketball. Without this constraint, unskilled players are encumbered by having to manoeuvre not only their own bodies but their bodies in relation to the basketball. Those players who embody efficient articulation with the basketball are able to exercise much more power in relation to opponents than those who do not.

Exhaustive Use

> [T]he 'mutual improvement school' was ... arranged as a machine to intensify the use of time ... [E]ach passing moment was filled with many different, but ordered activities; and ... the rhythm imposed by signals, whistles, orders imposed on everyone temporal norms that were intended both to accelerate the process of learning and to teach speed as a virtue.[39]

One of the ways I attempted to have some effect on the preparation of younger athletes in my community was to hold basketball camps in the summer for school-age girls. Each day these players were intensely caught up in a range of tightly scheduled activities including warm-up sessions, individual skills, weight training, conditioning, analysing skills on film, team practices, and scrimmages. The girls were organized in small groups and moved through a variety of different sites at a demanding pace in order not to alter the timetable of events for the day. We attempted to use up every moment of time available to us. This was, in part, to teach 'speed as a virtue,'[40] but also to 'extract ... from time, ever more available moments and, from each moment, ever more useful forces.'[41]

The timetable of daily practice is controlled to the extent that it ensures that athletes practice at the tempo expected in competition. Players must come to feel a bodily discomfort or feel 'unnatural' when they have not followed the temporal sequence and intensity for a particular skill and when skills and team play are not executed at the expected tempo. In order for players to achieve bodily discomfort because of improper sequencing or intensity, practice sessions must 'intensify the use of the slightest moment, as if time, in its very fragmentation, were inexhaustible or as if ... one could tend toward an ideal point at which one maintained maximum speed and efficiency.'[42]

Routinization and Embodiment of Exercise: 'The Organization of Geneses'

'The art of distributions' and 'the control of activity' include technologies (constraints) that penetrate individual bodies, enabling them to perform actions not otherwise possible. What Foucault refers to as 'the organization of geneses' involves the gradual progression and acquisition of knowledge in segments, building on each other and making possible coordination with others. Through repetitive, different, and graduated exercise, tasks are imposed on the body. Consequently, discipline not only analyses space and activities. It is a 'machinery for adding up and capitalizing time.'[43]

In the sections of *Discipline and Punish* on organization of geneses, Foucault describes the replacement of an apprenticeship system with a 'systematic, standardized, detailed and disciplined approach to knowledge and time'[44] that allows for 'development' and 'progression.' According to Foucault, there are four technologies that 'capitalize the time of individuals ... in a way that is susceptible to use and control'[45] and that together produce 'a matrix ... of activity through time, upon which a population and individuals within it may be located.'[46] These technologies enable 'the collective, permanent competition of individuals ... classified in relation to one another.'[47] This is an apt description of the preparatory and competition phases of high-performance sport. The four techniques include the following:

1. *Divide duration into successive or parallel segments, each of which must end at a specific time.*[48]

This technique separates the learning of a skill from its practice. 'Teach in turn posture, marching, the handling of weapons, shooting, and do not pass to another activity until the first has been completely mastered.'[49] The earlier description of reverse footwork and the reverse dribble is an example of the necessity of mastering one part of a skill before moving on to the next. I often referred to the 'building blocks' of basketball when talking about the progressive building of a team offence. The first building blocks were footwork and ball-handling skills, followed by manoeuvres of one offensive player against one defensive player and then 'elementary team play': two against two, three against three and four against four. Each of the 'blocks' was 'built' against progressively more intense defence.

Central to this first technology of the organization of geneses in disciplines like the army is the separation of the teaching of new recruits from the exercise of veterans. Coaches do often take advantage of homogeneous groupings if there is a wide gap in skill level among athletes. Seldom, however, is the skill difference between 'recruits' and veterans in high-performance sport so marked that separation of these two groups is required.

2. *Organize these threads according to an analytical plan – succession of elements as simple as possible, combining according to increasing complexity.*[50]

Consider the following adaptation of this technique from a basketball coaching text:[51]

We recommend a nine-step approach to installing an offensive system:
1. Teach your players the basic pattern or movement sequences by walking them through it until everyone is thoroughly familiar with it.
2. Drill the players in isolated segments of the basic pattern.
3. Add defense to the drill sequences.
4. Introduce options to the pattern one at a time in walk-through fashion.
5. Break down the options into drill segments.

6. Add passive defense to the options drill segments.
7. Practice the basic pattern, option, and automatics, first in breakdown drills and then in team form.
8. Add full-scale defense to the breakdown drills and team run-throughs.
9. Whenever you encounter problems, go back to the breakdown drills in practice.

Possibilities for offensive team play become embodied as a result of progressing with team-mates from the elementary to the complex. This also arranges and correlates a hierarchy of knowledge in terms of 'complexity' of knowledge in relation to time.[52]

3. *Finalise these temporal segments, decide on how long each will last and conclude it with an examination.*[53]

During team try-outs, coaches introduce selected skills over a period of designated time while determining which players have satisfactorily met the standard necessary for continued participation. Setting the time for try-outs, fixing those segments on which potential players will be assessed, and examining them on these has 'the triple function of showing whether the subject has reached the level required, of guaranteeing that each subject undergoes the same apprenticeship and of differentiating the abilities of each individual.'[54]

Athletes on teams may gain or lose opportunity to compete as a result of how they are assessed by coaches in practice sessions. Regularly scheduled competitions are also a form of examination that establish periods of time within which players are to gain competency in certain skills. How well an athlete performs in competition determines whether he or she will be permitted other competitive opportunities.

4. *Draw up series of series.*[55]

[L]ay down for each individual, according to his level, his seniority, his rank, the exercises that are suited to him; common exercises have a differing role and each difference involves specific exercises. At the end of each series, others begin, branch off and subdivide in turn. Thus each individual is caught up in a temporal series which specifically defines his level or his rank. It is a disciplinary polyphany of exercises.[56]

Preparation of athletes for a team sport like football, in which there are separate offensive and defensive squads, each with a number of highly specialized positions, requires an organization of activities for each practice session that both discipline an athlete in his requisite skills and identify him as occupying a particular position on the team in terms of his playing position and rank on the team. Thus, defensive teams, offensive teams, and special teams are engaged in skills specific to those teams. Quarterbacks, running backs, receivers, and linesmen are each engaged in specific exercises and within each of these groups less skilled athletes are engaged in activities to improve skill.

Synchronization of Team Play: 'The Composition of Forces'

[A] new demand appears to which discipline must respond: to construct a machine whose effect will be maximized by the concerted articulation of the elementary parts of which it is composed. Discipline is no longer simply an art of distributing bodies, of extracting time from them and accumulating it, but of composing forces in order to obtain an efficient machine.[57]

In team sports, the skills of individual players must be combined into an efficient unit 'whose effect [is] superior to the sum of [the abilities] that compose ... it ...'[58] A group of skilled individuals who are unable to integrate their skills with others will not constitute a successful team. According to Foucault, the composition of forces is achieved in the following ways:

1. *The individual body becomes an element that may be placed, moved, articulated on others.*[59]

Foucault quotes an 'ordonnance' that describes the training of soldiers first 'one by one, then two by two, then in greater numbers ... For the handling of weapons, one will ascertain that, when the soldiers have been separately instructed, they will carry it out two by two, and then change places alternately, so that the one on the left may learn to adapt himself to the one on the right.'[60]

Embodying the building blocks of team offence is not just a matter of learning skill in sequence. Players must be able to take any position in the sequence. In a sequence called the 'give and go,' for example, players must be able to pass and cut to the basket, but they must also be able to receive a pass and be able to pass it back to the cutting player.

2. *The various chronological series that discipline must combine to form a composite time are also pieces of machinery.*[61]

A skilled player knows how fast or quickly to move in a particular situation and still be in control. If a player cannot travel from one point to another and still be in control of his or her body and the basketball, then speed must be adjusted accordingly. In a team sport, players move in relation to team-mates and so they must incorporate an understanding of how quickly each player can move and stay in control. There is no advantage to being able to move very quickly, passing and cutting at great speed, if a team-mate has not managed to catch the ball thrown at this speed. Knowing how to adjust one's 'manoeuvrability speed' to others 'in such a way that the maximum quantity of forces may be extracted from each and combined with optimum results'[62] is another way in which time is embodied by athletes.

3. *This carefully measured combination of forces requires a precise system of command.*[63]

All the activity of the disciplined individual must be punctuated and sustained by injunctions whose efficacity rests on brevity and clarity; the order does not need to be explained or formulated; it must trigger off the required behaviour and that is enough.[64]

Once skills and team combinations are embodied, coaches rely on brief cues to signal that attention needs to be paid to some aspect of the team play or, during practice sessions, to move the team or segments of the team from drill to drill. The verbal cue 'confined space' signals a drill with which players are familiar and which they can begin without an explanation of what is involved in the drill; the cue 'block out' during a game or practice signals that players must pay attention to the details of this skill; the cue 'combination press' signals a move to a defensive transitional strategy. It is not necessary that players understand at an explicit or propositional level why the injunction[65] to do a particular skill or perform a particular strategy is to occur when it does; only that they 'perceive[e] the signal and react ... to it immediately.'[66]

Correct Training

Technologies that produce what Foucault calls docile bodies make it possible to identify and control *positions* or roles in relation to each other, but they do not make it possible to identify details about an individual other than that he or she is someone who is able to perform the skills associated with a position. What activities are to be performed by any individual in a particular space can be specified but *who* is performing the activity in the particular space cannot be specified through these technologies.

Information about who individuals are is provided by the technologies of 'correct training,' an art of strict discipline using 'simple instruments; hierarchal observation, normalizing judgement and their combination in a procedure that is specific to it, the examination.'[67] It is not enough for coaches to know how to distribute individuals in time and space, say, in an offensive system or to know how to developmentally produce athletic bodies to fit these roles. A coach must also know who is most skilled for a particular competition or situation. A central responsibility of coaches, then, is the assessment of athletic ability in order that the most skilled athletes compete when appropriate. Information about which athlete is most suitable for what position or situation is determined through examination, in which coaches observe athletes in relation to other athletes on the team and in relation to standards of performance for the sport. Through the coaches' observing and judging, comprehensive records of athletes' performances in training sessions and competitions are produced and the gaps between an athlete's performance and the standard for the activity are noted.

The effect of observation is not merely that athletes are seen. Observation makes it possible 'to know them; to alter them.'[68] With examinations coaches are able to assess how much work needs to be done to achieve a 'good' performance and to intervene to close the gap between an athlete's present performance and the desired performance. Observation and judgment are technologies of normalization because they implicate examined individuals in the project of closing the gap between their present performance and the 'norm' or standard for performance.

Through a 'normalizing judgment,' a coach assesses which athletes are better at which skills and rewards better players with playing opportunities. Athletes are as concerned as coaches to 'norm the nonstandard'[69] because of the lure of being rewarded by more competitive opportunities and perhaps by fame of some kind. 'Conformity is rewarded with applause and fame; neglect is punished with poor test results, the shame of defeat, and extra training sessions.'[70] There are, then, other effects of the examination of athletes in addition to knowledge of individual athletes. Normalization and homogenization are an effect of the 'constant pressure [for athletes] to conform to the same model, so that they might all be ... like one another.'[71] As Heikkala indicates, 'normalization ... means conformity to the 'rationale' of both training and competing according to the plans made (by the coach) and conformity to the institutional forms, customs, and rules of sport.'[72]

The disciplinary technologies of high-performance sport are constraints placed on the actions of athletes. This exercise of power by coaches produces skills that athletes require for performance. Skilled athletes, in turn, constrain other athletes' actions during competition and, in doing so, exercise power. Perhaps paradoxically, the more constrained an athlete is by a discipline, the more 'choice' he or she actually has within the discipline. For example, there are a number of ways in which a basketball team can attempt to score against an opponent. Often teams utilize pre-planned 'plays' in which players move in a prescribed sequence in relation to each other. More disciplined teams – that is, teams with more highly developed skills – may use what is called a passing game, in which player movement is not pre-set but is based on some basic principles with a series of contingencies – 'if this, then that' possibilities. Basic principles in the passing game include provision for defensive floor balance and rebounding balance as well as rules about passing the basketball, the use of post players, and the number of players in the key area at any one time. A simple example of a contingency might be that *if* a player cutting through the key does not receive a pass, *then* post up on the lane; *if* still no pass, *then* set an offside screen, *then* move into the periphery as a possible outlet in the event that the ball is reversed.

In order to have some success with the passing game, not only must players be able to perform skills at a high level of proficiency, they must be able to recognize where both team-mates and opponents are on the court and to understand the activities in which these players are engaged. It takes years of exposure to the disciplinary technologies of the sport of basketball to acquire this set of skills. These disciplinary technologies make it possible for skilled athletes to 'choose' from a number of movement possibilities and perform what seems to be the best alternative. Players who are not superbly controlled by the discipline of high-performance basketball would not be able to make these choices.

The Coach in the Athlete: Panopticism

> He who is subjected to a field of visibility, and who knows it, assumes responsibility for the constraints of power; he makes them play spontaneously upon himself; he inscribes in himself the power relation in which he simultaneously plays both roles; he becomes the principle of his own subjection.[73]

Conformity takes hold of an athlete, in part, because he or she is visible. Realizing that they can be seen by coaches, athletes come to monitor their own behaviour and shape it according to the expectations of the sport. In effect, the watchful eye of the coach and the normalizing standards of the sport become embodied by the athlete. Foucault refers to this embodiment of the gaze of authority as 'panopticism' – 'a generalizable model of functioning; a way of defining power relations in terms of the everyday life of men.'[74]

The notion of panopticism was derived by Foucault from the Panopticon, an architectural design for a prison produced by the philosopher and prison reformer Jeremy Bentham. Bentham's Panopticon was an architectural figure consisting of a tower at its centre with windows looking out at a building divided into cells. Each individual in these cells is seen by the supervisor in the tower and prevented from seeing either the supervisor or those in the other cells. 'He is seen, but he does not see.'[75] Because of the structure of the tower, the prisoner is unable to tell whether he is watched and consequently has a feeling of constant surveillance. The awareness that one may be watched leads to an internalization of the gaze and a policing of one's own behaviour. The inmate becomes his own guard.

Panopticism 'is polyvalent in its applications; it serves to reform prisoners, but also to treat patients, to instruct schoolchildren, to confine the insane, to supervise workers, to put beggars and idlers to work ... Whenever one is dealing with a multiplicity of individuals on whom a task or a particular form of behaviour must be imposed, the panoptic schema may be used.'[76] John Fiske describes how female workers at a Trans World Airlines reservation centre are 'known' and conform through a panoptic gaze: 'The room in which she sits is a vast hundred-foot-square enclosure ... [further] divided into the 350 work stations which are occupied by the 350 bodies ... Each station is equipped with a telephone headset, a chair and a computer terminal ... In the centre of the enclosure is a small glass-walled one in which the supervisor sits. She monitors the 350 bodies visually and electronically, for each telephone line is connected, not just to the outside world, but to her.'[77]

In high-performance sport, training sessions are organized so that all athletes in the session can be seen by a coach or coaches and so that athletes are constantly engaged in activity. Athletes are unaware of when they are actually watched yet know that this is always possible. Since less than intense participation in practice sessions often leads to some kind of punishment, the worst of which would be fewer or no opportunities for competition, high-performance athletes come to understand that it is in their best interest to train with intensity. The effects of panopticism are visceral. When athletes perform skills incorrectly or without intensity, the movement feels 'wrong' or 'unnatural.' Self-policing the intensity of personal training is done not only to avoid punishment. Like those who police their own behaviour with respect to drinking and driving because they have taken on the values of 'good' citizenry, high-performance athletes police their own behaviours because they have incorporated both the technologies and values of docility and correct training.

Random or 'unannounced' testing of high-performance athletes for banned performance-enhancing drugs is intended to serve as a panopticon. The hope is that athletes will police themselves when they know that they can be tested (watched) at any time. As a brochure from the then Canadian Centre for Drug-free Sport (CCDS) makes clear, 'This means that the tests are unscheduled and you will not know you are going to be tested until: you are contacted by the CCDS and are requested to appear at a Doping Control station within thirty-six (36) hours (short notice testing); an authorized Certified Doping Control Officer (sample collection officer) arrives at your training or competition venue and presents you with an official Athlete Selection Order (no notice testing).'[78]

Random drug testing doesn't always succeed as a panoptic device because technologies have been developed to neutralize the test. As I explore in chapter 4, equally compelling to athletes is the uncertainty of whether rivals are utilizing neutralizing technologies to gain an advantage.

Sport Discipline and Knowing-Known Bodies

Most of this chapter has detailed how sport discipline controls bodies through the organization of time, space, and modality of movement and through examinations. I want to say more about the subject matter of high-performance sport and its communication through discourse. The subject matter of the discipline of high-performance sport includes propositional knowledge about the biomechanics of movement, the physiology of high performance, the methods and results of conditioning and training, the care and prevention of athletic injuries, motor control, the psychology of learning and performing, nutrition, the pedagogy of learning and performing, and, of course, sport skills and competitive strategies. Texts in the physiology of high performance include among other things information about the aerobic and anaerobic systems during rest and exercise, the energy cost of exercise, the overload principle, and body composition assessment.[79] Biomechanics texts explain forces and movement, body torque and rotation, body balance and stability control, force and motion relations, linear momentum, kinetic energy, and angular momentum.[80] Table 2.2 is an example of 'knowledge' about the acquisition of movement skills taken from a text in motor control.[81]

As these few examples illustrate, propositional knowledges that inform the technologies of high-performance sport are wide ranging even while concerned with minute detail. Coaches utilize knowledge generated by the discipline or subject matter of high-performance sport and translate this information into ever more exacting technologies of docility to produce ever more disciplined athletes.

The discipline of high-performance sport produces two types of experts: highly skilled athletes who know how to perform rarified skills and scientists and coaches who through discourse are able to convey complex propositional knowledges about athletic performance. To be an expert of either type, one must incorporate values of the discipline and be subjected to disciplinary technologies that produce expertise. For athletes this involves subjection to the technologies generated by sport and

TABLE 2.2 The Learner

coaching science. Scientists and coaches are subjected to the study and interpretation of athlete performance, to extended practice in the controlled space, time, and modality of the laboratory, and to a panopticism that observes and compares according to expert standards. As Fiske writes of the supervisor of the TWA reservation centre: 'She may be a slightly larger cog in the machine, through which its power passes to the 350, smaller cogs, but she is still a cog. Her movements are locked into theirs; the machine holds her in place as precisely as it does them. Her behaviours are as closely monitored as theirs.'[82] Like the supervisor of the TWA reservation centre, coaches, scientists, and Certified Doping Control Officers are as implicated in the machinery of conformity as are athletes. They are just slightly larger cogs.

Confessional Technology

In the last chapter I commented that the propositional knowledges of scientists and coaches have more value than the procedural knowledges of athletes.[83] This is not to say that what scientists and coaches *do* is more valued than what athletes do but that, in a hierarchy of knowledge, propositional knowledges have more currency even in a context in which every aspect of the discipline is focused on producing better athletic performance. What athletes do may be more important than what coaches do but what coaches and sport scientists say is much more important than what athletes say. Coaches and sport scientists control the subject matter and hence the discourse of what counts as legitimate talk[84] about high-performance sport and in doing so establish themselves as uniquely knowledgeable speakers.

Even though what athletes do is much more important than what they say, the value placed on propositional knowledge often implicates athletes in technologies that are designed to encourage athletes to translate their bodily 'know-how' into explicit propositional terms through 'self-talk,'[85] mental imaging, and 'attentional style' profiles. The attempt to translate procedural knowledge into propositional terms provides sport psychologists and coaches with additional information about athletes so that they can intervene to improve performance. Another effect of this 'self-talk' is that athletes come to understand their own performances and their identities *as* athletes in propositional terms. Confessional technology encourages individuals to report their experiences of performing and contributes to the construction of particular ways of understanding athletic identities. 'The confessional operates through ... the individual's acknowledgement of his or her own actions and thoughts ... It is a process which confirms identity. Through the act of speaking, the self is constituted, tied to self-knowledge.'[86]

To get at what is at stake when coaches and sport psychologists assume a responsibility to elicit and interpret the 'self-talk' of athletes, it is necessary to leave *Discipline and Punish* and turn to Foucault's *History of Sexual-*

ity, Volume I: An Introduction. In *The History of Sexuality*, Foucault describes the uses that have been made of the confessional to make it possible for people to achieve self-knowledge as sexual subjects. A confession is made in the presence of an 'authority who requires the confession, prescribes and appreciates it, and intervenes in order to judge, punish, forgive, console, and reconcile ... and [to] ... produce ... intrinsic modifications in the person who articulates it.'[87] Implicit in the confession of experience is the assumption that self-knowledge can be attained by confessing to experts who interpret the confession. Also implicit is the assumption that it is possible to improve the confessor by therapeutic, normalizing interventions by experts.

In the early 1980s I was interested in the attention-control training (ACT) developed by Robert Nideffer as a possible means to improve player performance. My decision to take up ACT, which is still a central part of the coaching certification program of the Coaching Association of Canada, implicated athletes in a number of activities outside of the gymnasium. Through a paper-and-pencil test athletes indicated their responses to a variety of possibly stressful situations.

> By your answering a number of questions about how you have functioned in the past, it's possible for us to conclude to some degree of accuracy what your attentional strengths and weaknesses are ... If ... you indicate that you make mistakes because you concentrate on one player and forget about what other players are doing, I know that you can narrow attention, but are unable to broaden it, and when a broad focus is demanded, you have difficulty. With this kind of information, plus additional knowledge about your level of anxiety, I can suggest procedures for you to use to learn to broaden your attention.[88]

Based on expert interpretation of the questionnaires, remedial techniques were introduced, including breathing exercises, 'centring,' and exercises to control focus of attention, so that athletes could perform better in situations that required particular attentional abilities. Athletes came to understand themselves in terms of their attentional abilities – as confident, hesitant, or aggressive, or as 'chokers.'

A 'confession' of 'attentional style' is only one of the ways in which a coach or a sport psychologist encourages athletes to put their 'know-how' about performance into words. An exercise I regularly presented to athletes involved their telling or writing how they would respond to specific competitive situations. Here is an excerpt from one list of situations:

i) You have passed the ball to the post side forward and your defender jumps to the weak side of the screen set by the forward cutting high.
ii) You have rebounded the ball and both the outlet to the side and to the middle are contested.
iii) You are defending a player who is near the foul line when you see a team mate leave her defensive assignment to double team the ball at midcourt.

Players were to say or write how they were expected to perform and I then interpreted their responses as an indication of their understanding of team systems. I then used this information to intervene with 'remedial' drills in practice sessions.

Here I do some confessing of my own: while I was aware that an ability to describe the appropriate response to a competitive situation wasn't the same as an ability to perform the response, and I was aware that there were some players who could perform but could not translate the performance into words, I nevertheless believed that my control of competitive situations could be enhanced the more I could get players to talk. This was a self-fulfilling belief: by using confessional technology, it was possible for me to 'discover' players' 'attentional control' and their abilities to understand team systems and then interpret this information to make decisions about disciplinary technologies. For example, if I 'discovered' that a player had a narrow focus of attention, it was possible for me to structure training sessions so that cues which required attention were emphasized and repeated. My interpretation of athletes' 'confessions' produced another set of coaching imperatives and a number of directives to change players in ways that I believed were more productive of competitive success. Confessional technology, then, was used to validate my interventionist expertise.

This completes the mapping onto high-performance sport of the features of modern disciplinary power as described by Foucault. I have undertaken this task in order to demonstrate how athletes are produced by modern power and how they become knowable as athletes to experts and to themselves. What should be apparent from this account is that sport at the millennium is still very much a modern project. The context in which high-performance athletes are produced has changed, however. While the production of skilled, 'masterful' high-performance athletes remains a modern project, high-performance sport now occurs in a postmodern context, a context that, among other things, questions 'the legitimacy of mastery'[89] and that is 'irreducibly and irrevocably pluralistic, split into a multitude of sovereign units and sites of authority, with no horizontal or vertical order, either in actuality or potency.'[90]

As Michael Real points out, 'the first modern [Olympic] Games in Athens in 1896 featured neither women [athletes] nor athletes from outside Europe and North America.'[91] More than a hundred years later, there have been shifts from 'aristocratic to commercial support [for sport], from upper-class to diverse participation, and from male European and American domination to female and global involvement.'[92] In this postmodern context of diversity, technologies designed to discipline athletes are complicated by other processes of identity formation. The 'de-Europeanized and postpatriarchal diversity of athletes'[93] has opened up spaces in modern sport for what might be called postmodern interventions. In the next chapter, I explore how processes of 'gender,' 'sexuality,' and 'race' confound modern athletic identity and, consequently, the demands of modern sport, so that in the last chapter I will be able to explore postmodern interventions.

CHAPTER THREE

Hybrid Athletes

Discipline takes hold of bodies by filling in gaps in time, space, and modality of movement. Organization of time, space, and movement constitute the technologies or constraints of docility that coaches utilize to close gaps between unskilled performance and the competitive standards for their sport. Technologies of discipline may also extend beyond the production of skill to other aspects of an athlete's life, placing restrictions on what athletes eat, when they sleep, other activities in which they are engaged, and with whom they associate. Yet, even with the encroachment of sport discipline into time, space, and movement outside practice and competition sites, athletes are not homogeneous. The relentlessness of discipline, particularly for adult athletes, can never completely eradicate gaps in skill or completely close the gaps between athletic life and life outside sport.

Despite the detail of sport discipline, athlete identity is not consumed by it. Athletes, like other people, participate in a number of overlapping, conflicting disciplines that together produce a distinctive hybrid identity for each person. This hybridity guarantees that there will always be gaps in athletic identity – gaps that can be exploited when it is necessary to refuse the homogenizing impulses of modern sport.

Since the processes of modern sport now occur in a postmodern context of diversity in which athletes are hybrids of gender, sexuality, race, and ability, I am interested in looking at the implications for modern sport when hybrid athletes are faced with the demands of sport discipline. I am interested in making the case that gender, sexuality, and race are also disciplines with their own set of performances and performance standards that are also constrained by technologies of docility and correct training.

Establishing gender, sexuality, and race as disciplines is not as straightforward as establishing high-performance sport as a discipline. Sport has acknowledged experts, controlled training sessions, and specific sites for performing and examining skills. Rebounding, for example, is performed and assessed only in the context of a basketball game or practice session. Knowing how to interact with athletes outside an athletic context does not require athletes to be known as athletes because other skills are required for these contexts. Every enclosure, on the other hand, is a site for disciplining bodies by gender, sexuality, and race. If someone does not perform, say, gender skills as a notification of one's sex in all situations, others are baffled or even angered. As philosopher Marilyn Frye writes, 'We are socially and communicatively helpless if we do not know the sex of everybody we have anything to do with.'[1] The sex of those we encounter is always apparent because each of us performs required skills and behaviours that announce (or lie about) our genitalia.

I realize that, by attempting to map disciplinary technologies onto gender, sexuality, and race, I risk homogenizing them as separate categories. Utilizing the work of Paul Willis, Jean Grimshaw makes it clear that conceptions of masculinity, for example, vary according to class: a conception of masculinity held by working-class boys included a belief that anything other than manual labour was sissy, including academic or book work.[2] Grimshaw compared Willis's work with Hudson's 1966 study of English public schoolboys, which showed that these boys did not have contempt for academic work, although they regarded certain forms of intellectual activity, particularly science, to be more masculine than others.[3] The challenge is to talk about processes that construct identity without privileging, in the case of gender, a particular racialized, classed, or sexualized version of identity.

By attempting to establish that gender, sexuality, and race are disciplines that may conflict with sport discipline, I also risk consolidating as natural the very categories that I want to show are constructed through disciplinary discourses and technologies. To contend with this tension, my focus is placed on processes that create identities rather than on the experiences of those already categorized. As Joan Scott writes, 'We need to attend to the historical processes that, through discourse, position subjects and produce their experiences.'[4]

This attention to processes that produce experiences of identity is not yet the preferred approach of social scientists of sport. More often, a social scientist of sport starts with a category, say, the category 'the female athlete,' with the goal of describing her experiences. By approaching the question in this way, the social scientist already presumes to know who a female athlete is, thus contributing to the solidification of the category 'the female athlete.' Finding representatives of this category, and then collecting accounts of experiences that fit this categorization is 'the bedrock of evidence upon which explanation is built. Questions about the constructed nature of experience, about how subjects are constituted as different in the first place ... are left aside.'[5] An assumption that there are common experiences of 'female athletes' posits a standard or normal set of experiences for female athletes, making 'other' experiences exceptional accounts. A disabled female athlete, a black female athlete, or a lesbian athlete are, then, necessarily produced as 'other' to the norm of 'the female athlete.'

Experiences of 'female athletes' don't just happen. These experiences are the consequences of certain sets of discourses and technologies that make possible these experiences and not others. Tracing discourses and technologies of disciplines that have produced experiences of 'athlete,' 'female,' and, say, 'white,' 'able-bodied,' or 'heterosexual,' make it possible to explore how these discourses and technologies differentiate and how they create the fact of different social groups in the first place.

In *Discipline and Punish,* Foucault traced discourses and technologies that produced disciplined imprisoned bodies and the category 'prisoner'; those that produced disciplined workplace bodies and the category 'worker'; and those that produced disciplined schooled bodies and the category 'student.' Similarly, in the previous chapter, I traced discourses and technologies that produce disciplined athletic bodies and the category or identity of 'athlete.' Genealogy is the name Foucault gave to uncovering processes that produce experiences that consolidate identity. In this chapter I want to complicate the genealogy of 'the athlete' undertaken in the last chapter by surfacing other discourses and technologies that differentially produce experiences among athletes and thereby produce variations of 'the athlete.'

In introducing diversity as a complication for sport discipline, I do not want to lose sight of the fact that each discipline, including gender, sexuality, and race, have standards according to which individuals are assessed and normalized. Even while disciplines overlap and confound each other, it is necessary to be reminded of Foucault's contention that modern disciplines have produced a '*society of normalisation*'[6] in which there is 'constant pressure to conform to the same model, so that they might all be ... like one another.'[7]

A notion of 'the normal' signifying that which conforms to and does not deviate from a standard coincided with developments in statistics and probability theory during the nineteenth century.[8] Before the nineteenth century there were no concepts of normal and abnormal bodies.[9] Instead there was a concept of an ideal person and body type in comparison to which all human beings were lacking. The word 'normal' signifying that which conforms to and does not deviate from a standard only enters the English language around 1840, coinciding with developments in statistics and probability during the nineteenth century.[10]

Key to the conceptualization of the 'normal' to signify what is usual or typical was the work of statistician Adolphe Quetelet. Quetelet proposed that the method astronomers used to locate a star – the 'law of error' – could be applied to frequency distributions of human and social phenomena. Astronomers found that most sightings of a star fell in the centre of a bell curve. They considered those sightings that fell to the sides of the curve to be errors. According to Quetelet, physical characteristics as well as moral and social behaviours could be plotted and determined utilizing this 'law of error.' Quetelet constructed the notion of the 'average man' from the 'true mean' of human attributes.[11] He thought the average or the 'normal' to signify not only what is usual or typical but also the way things ought to be. In contrast, 'errors' were abnormalities, deviations, or extremes.[12] Establishment of the 'normal' as the typical and the 'good' made it possible to compare people and isolate those who deviated from the norm, and for experts to intervene through attempts to 'norm the nonstandard.'[13]

The norm divides the population into standard and non-standard subpopulations while establishing deviations or extremes.[14] Quetelet wrote, for example, that 'deviations more or less great from the mean have constituted ... ugliness in body as well as vice in morals and a state of sickness with regard to the constitution.'[15] The idea that there is a normal body to which the 'abnormal' should aspire leaves no tolerance for variation or difference from this norm.[16] The social construction of normalcy is, then, what creates the 'problem' of the disabled person,[17] the unfeminine woman, the feminized man, the homosexual, 'white trash,' the 'oversexed' black man, 'the delinquent,' and 'the deviant,' as well as 'the excellent,' 'the good,' 'the proper,' and all other categorizations established by measurement against a norm or standard, including, I will argue, 'the ethical.'

While Quetelet's focus was on central tendencies, Sir Francis Galton, founder of the biometric school of statistical research, was interested in distributions and deviations from the mean.[18] And, while Quetelet considered average or 'normal' human characteristics to be how things ought to be, Galton regarded the 'normal' as an indication of mediocrity requiring improvement.[19] Galton thought it problematic to consider all extremes in human characteristics as errors or abnormalities.[20] Certain attributes valued by him, such as tallness, intelligence, ambitiousness, strength, and fertility should be regarded as positive distributions of a trait and not errors. Galton divided the bell curve (renamed the normal distribution curve) into quartiles that established a ranking system for characteristics. Distributions around the norm were no longer regarded as equal: the average, now referred to as the median, represented mediocrity. Those in the lower quartile were posited as deviant or abnormal and as objects of intervention, while those in the upper quartile represented progress, perfectibility, and the elimination of abnormality.[21]

Quetelet's appropriation of the 'law of error' to explain stability in social statistics and Galton's imposition of his values about human development onto the bell curve have had profound effects on what is understood as normal and abnormal. Far from being a neutral, objective enterprise, statistics is a discourse that has produced social meaning about 'normalcy' and 'abnormalcy,' 'ability' and 'disability,' influenced the creation of categories such as 'the intelligent,' 'the deviant,' and 'the disabled,' and supported differentiation of 'normal' behaviours by gender, sexuality, race, class, and ability in many different social contexts from classrooms to playgrounds, from boardrooms to factory floors. Notions such as 'success,' 'competence,' 'excellence,' 'merit,' and 'ability' acquire meaning only in contexts in which some skills, attributes, or characteristics are valued more than are others. Indeed, McDermott and Varenne go as far as to say that '[c]ompetence is a fabrication, a mock-up ... [and] the most arbitrary tasks can be [contrived as] the measure of individual development.'[22]

The legitimacy of categories created and supported by statistics has been reinforced when these categories are used to find confirming cases. What counts as 'the normal' and deviations from the normal are defined in advance and then, given those definitions, experts isolate and deal with anomalies.[23] This intervention by experts is based on the 'central insight of statistics [which] is the idea that a population can be normed.'[24] Yet, the impetus to 'norm the non-standard' depends upon an assumption that there are normal bodies and normal abilities existing independently, rather than as a result of the discourse of statistics.

'Norming the non-standard' also relies upon and ensures the place of experts who can intervene to make bodies or abilities 'better.' An example of the tyranny of the norm and the place of experts in assuring this tyranny is advice columnist Ann Landers's reply to a mother who wrote in despair at the thoughtlessness of people who stare at her nine-year-old daughter, who has a port-wine birthmark on her face. Landers advised immediate consultation with an expert on laser therapy to lighten the stain. 'Instead of trying to change people,' Landers wrote, 'please take steps at once to get rid of that albatross around your child's neck.'[25]

In the sections that follow I discuss discourses and technologies that attempt to normalize people into identity categories. I focus on gender, sexuality, race, and ability while touching on class in each of them.

Discourses and Technologies of Gender

In her essay 'Throwing Like a Girl: A Phenomenology of Feminine Body Comportment and Spatiality,' first published in 1980, Iris Young cites the 1966 work of Erwin Straus, who commented on the 'remarkable difference in the manner of throwing of the two sexes.'[26] Straus observed that 'girls do not bring their whole bodies into the motion as much as the boys. They do not reach back, twist, move backward, step, and lean forward. Rather, the girls tend to remain relatively immobile except for their arms, and even the arm is not extended as far as it could be.'[27]

Boys, as David Whitson points out, 'are encouraged to experience their bodies, and therefore themselves, in forceful, space-occupying, even dominating ways ... [A]ssertiveness and confidence, as ways of relating to others, become embodied through the development of strength and skill and through prevailing over opponents in competitive situations.'[28] 'Boys are taught that to endure pain is courageous, to survive pain is manly';[29] that their bodies are weapons;[30] that 'to be an adult male is distinctly to occupy space, to have a physical presence in the world.'[31]

Young comments that 'many of the observed differences between men and women in the performance of tasks requiring coordinated strength are due not so much to brute muscular strength, but to the way each sex *uses* the body in approaching tasks.'[32] 'Not only is there a typical style of throwing like a girl, but there is a more or less typical style of running like a girl, climbing like a girl, swinging like a girl, hitting like a girl. They have in common, first, that the whole body is not put into fluid and directed motion, but rather, in swinging and hitting, for example, the motion is concentrated in one body part; and second, that the woman's motion tends not to reach, extend, lean, stretch, and follow through in the direction of her intention.'[33]

These accounts are not of 'natural' differences. Indeed, as Michael Messner comments, 'throwing "like a girl" is actually a more anatomically natural motion for the human arm. Throwing "like a man" is a learned action ... . an unnatural act, an act that ... must be learned.'[34] Disciplined athletic bodies are not 'natural' or 'normal,' and there is nothing 'natural' or 'normal' about a body disciplined as feminine or masculine. Femininity and masculinity, like sport skills, are acts or performances that must be learned.

Young acknowledges that many of the differences between females and males in embodied skills stem from the fact that girls and women have not been exposed to sport discipline. 'For the most part, girls and women are not given the opportunity to use their full bodily capacities in free and open engagement with the world, nor are they encouraged as much as boys to develop specifically bodily skills.'[35] As important, however, as these differences are the consequences of practising or repeating 'feminine' gestures and movements. As Young writes, '[T]he modalities of feminine bodily existence are not merely privative ... and thus their source is not merely in lack of practice, though this is certainly an important element.' She goes on to say that 'the girl learns actively to hamper her movements ... In assuming herself as a girl, she takes herself up as fragile ... When I was about thirteen, I spent hours practicing a "feminine" walk which was stiff, closed, and rotated from side to side.'[36]

Children who do not practise appropriate gender skills may be pathologized and sent by parents and teachers to experts for remedial work. Many North American hospitals have Gender Identity Disorder clinics to treat children diagnosed with 'Gender Identity Disorder,' which is regarded as a 'pathology involving the Core Gender Identity ... consistent with one's biological sex.'[37] In *Gender Shock*, Phyllis Burke describes the behaviour modification of children who do not conform to expectations for their assigned gender. Seven-year-old Becky, for example, was identified as having 'female sexual identity disturbance'[38] because she 'liked to stomp around with her pants tucked into her cowboy boots, and she refused to wear dresses. She liked basketball and climbing ... She liked to play with her toy walkie-talkies, rifle, dart game and marbles. She stood with her hands on her hips, fingers facing forward. She swung her arms, and took big, surefooted strides when she walked.'[39] The 'cure' for Becky's 'gender identity disorder' consisted of one hundred and two sessions of behaviour modification in the clinic and ninety-six sessions in her bedroom. She was rewarded for accepting 'feminine sex-typed' toys and behaviour and rejecting 'masculine sex-typed' toys and behaviour.[40]

As Burke indicates, 'rather than being "cured," Becky's self-esteem was destroyed' by constant monitoring. 'Her ... desires and feelings had been worn down, split off from her everyday world, only to become hidden within a secret and shamed place inside her. Becky valiantly strove for acceptance and to do what was necessary in the face of overwhelming odds. She wanted to earn back love, and if that meant choosing the pots and pans over the soft-ball mitt, so be it.'[41] A desire to cooperate, a typically 'feminine' behaviour, overrode Becky's desire to play with 'masculine sex-typed' toys and she was forced or normalized into one of two manifestations of gender.

'Throwing like a girl' is obviously, then, not merely the result of not practising to throw 'like a boy.' Throwing, walking, sitting, standing, and gesturing like a girl are produced by the repetition of techniques that discipline femininity and make femininity feel 'natural' and 'normal.' In 'Foucault, Femininity, and the Modernization of Patriarchal Power,' Sandra Bartky details some of the disciplinary practices or technologies that go into producing femininity, 'practices that produce a body which in gesture and appearance is recognizably feminine.'[42] While it is not my intention to itemize these details, practices familiar in North American culture are those that produce particular ways of walking, standing, sitting, and getting in and out of vehicles, and that over time produce particular facial expressions. These gestures, movements, and expressions are embodied as a result of daily, disciplined repetition. And, like the embodiment of sport skills, improper or inadequate performance of required feminine skills feels 'wrong' or 'unnatural' to the performer.

Practising femininity requires an 'investment of time, the use of a wide variety of preparations, the mastery of a set of techniques and ... the acquisition of a specialized knowledge.'[43] Much of this specialized knowledge is an embodied knowledge about the manipulation of a variety of cosmetic tools, including 'the blow dryer, styling brush, curling iron, hot curlers, wire curlers, eye-liner, lipliner, lipstick brush, eyelash curler, mascara brush.'[44] Like disciplined athletes, feminine women are highly skilled.[45] To criticize women for embodying skills of the discipline of femininity is to threaten these 'women with a certain de-skilling.'[46] Feminine women are rewarded for conforming to standards of femininity, but they are also limited because they are often unable to participate in skills that are considered standards of competency in a culture, including skills of sport.

An individual's femininity or masculinity is measured or examined against conventional standards, represented in popular media and reinforced by schools, families, religions, medicine, the law, and other institutions. Those whose bodies do not match the standard – that is, the bodies of almost everyone – may turn to expert intervention to remedy their 'deficiencies.' 'How to become healthier, fitter, thinner, and more attractive are recurring themes with variations' in both general women's magazines and in fitness magazines for women.[47] Margaret Duncan argues that the way in which these themes are framed makes them 'panoptic mechanisms' – mechanisms that, she says, invite 'a continual self-conscious body monitoring in women.'[48] Little wonder that body altering is a multi-billion-dollar business in North America. Dieticians, electrolysists, cosmetic surgeons, fitness instructors, weight trainers, and make-up professionals assist individuals' attempts to achieve the standard or normal gendered body. 'All these experts provide services that can be bought; all these experts are perceived as administering and transforming the human body into an increasingly artificial and ever more perfect object.'[49]

Notwithstanding, or perhaps because of, overlapping and often conflicting representations of femininity and masculinity, there is an 'everyday stress and anxiety' about how one performs one's gender that produces bodies habituated to self-monitoring and self-normalization.[50] This internalized panopticon is not only embodied by girls and women. 'It isn't only size which provokes anxieties about the body among teenage boys. There is the question of shape. Pubescent, I was quite convinced I was brutally ugly, that my ears stuck out, my face was misshapen, that other people could hardly bear to look at me. There is also the question of clumsiness ... But more important, these anxieties have a great deal to do with the physical definition of oneself as male.'[51]

While most girls and women are not formally trained in femininity unless enrolled in, say, 'charm' schools, or unless, like Becky, they have been sent by parents to a Gender Identity Disorder clinic, organized sport is a central context within which masculine gestures and movements are practised and normalized. According to Whitson, in societies in which less value is attached to physical prowess, 'sport has become ... one of the central sites in the social production of masculinity.'[52]

Feminine girls and women are ill-equipped for sport because they have not practised sport skills *and* because they *have* practised feminine skills. Boys who have practised 'conventional masculinity,'[53] but have not practised sport skills will do better than girls who have practised 'femininity' and not practised sport skills, because to practise masculinity is to practise 'forceful, space-occupying' movements – movements that are also important for sport participation. A boy who is not skilled at conventional masculinity may have similar difficulties in a sport environment to those of a feminine girl, while a girl who has practised sport skills and also practised feminine skills is faced with a situation with which a masculine boy in sport is not. She must contend with a conflict between the requisite skills of femininity and the requisite skills of sport.

To say that someone 'throws like a girl' is to critique his or her poor throwing technique, while to say that someone (always a girl or woman) 'throws like a boy' is intended to compliment her. A girl or woman who 'throws like a boy' has properly practised the skill, while a girl or boy, woman or man who 'throws like a girl' has not had this practice. 'Throwing like a boy' does not, however, only mean that the thrower throws correctly. 'Throwing like a boy' also means that the thrower throws in a way that is consistent with bodily comportment and movement disciplined through repetition of masculinity. Since this is the case, a girl in sport must not only practise sport skills, she must practise 'masculine' skills. While there is nothing normal about an athletic body for either men or women, male athletic embodiment is an ideal of masculinity, and female athletic embodiment is a contradiction.

Gender and Docility

> If boys simply grew into men and that was that, the efforts described to teach boys how to be men would be redundant. We can suggest, then, that 'becoming a man' is something that boys (and especially adolescent boys) work at.[54]
>
> The disciplinary techniques through which the 'docile bodies' of women are constructed aim at a regulation which is perpetual and exhaustive – a regulation of the body's size and contours, its appetite, posture, gestures, and general comportment in space and the appearance of each of its visible parts.[55]

Bartky notes that Foucault pays no attention 'to those disciplines that produce a modality of embodiment that is particularly feminine.'[56] She goes on to say that, by assuming that 'men and women [bear] the same relationship to the characteristic institutions of modern life,'[57] the subject of Foucault's projects is male by default. Technologies of conventional masculinity were not specified by Foucault apart from those that produce the male worker, the male soldier, and the schoolboy. When Bartky provides detail for conventional femininity, we are left with the impression that there are many more disciplinary practices for femininity than masculinity and, consequently, that feminine women are more docile than masculine men.

While both Whitson and Bartky understand gender to be socially constructed, Whitson attributes this construction to something boys and men work at, while Bartky implies that girls and women are passive recipients of some constructive force. Indeed, Bartky writes that 'disciplinary practises ... engender the 'docile bodies' of women ... more docile than the bodies of men.'[58]

The superior value attributed to 'masculine' skills, even though also acquired by discipline, makes it possible to represent the disciplined docility of femininity, but not of masculinity, as passivity. As Monique Deveaux writes, 'Bartky's use of the docile bodies thesis has the effect of diminishing and delimiting women's subjectivity, at times treating women as robotic receptacles of culture rather than as active agents who are both constituted by, and reflective, of their social and cultural contexts.'[59]

Discourses and Technologies of Sexuality

One of the central projects of North American academic feminism in the 1970s and 1980s was to debunk scientific and social-scientific work that linked biology and social position by distinguishing between sex as naturally occurring and gender as culturally acquired.[60] By taking seriously this distinction between sex and gender, it is not possible to attribute 'the values or social functions of women [or men] to biological necessity' nor is it possible to 'refer to natural or unnatural gendered behavior.'[61] Masculinity and femininity can appear on any body – there is no 'natural' home for either.

The persistence of the perception that gender is natural is part of a larger assumption that links together sex, gender, sexual practice, and desire.[62] To disrupt this link requires not only a denaturalization of gender but a denaturalization of sex, sexual practice, and sexual desire as well. Without this disruption, gender, even though conceived as an effect of culture, can still be 'inscribed on anatomically differentiated bodies, where those bodies are understood as passive recipients of an inexorable cultural law.'[63] 'Woman' will continue to be inscribed on a fixed notion of female embodiment and 'man' will continue to be inscribed on a fixed notion of male embodiment.

Judith Butler argues that what it means to be sexed as female or male arises from gender performances.[64] What counts as a male or female body is a result of repetitive performances of gendered gestures, movements, and comportment.[65] Even though all human bodies have permeable orifices and appendages that can penetrate these orifices, the openness and forcefulness of masculine comportment suggest a body that is impermeable, forceful, and strong, while the closed passivity of feminine comportment suggests a body that is permeable and penetratable.

Commenting on the photographs of masculine and feminine body posture by photographer Marianne Wex, Sandra Bartky notes the following: 'Women sit waiting for trains with arms close to the body, hands folded together in their laps, toes pointing straight ahead and turned inward, and legs pressed together. The women in these photographs make themselves small and narrow, harmless; they seem tense; they take up little space. Men, on the other hand, expand into the available space; they sit with legs far apart and arms flung out at some distance from the body. Most common in these sitting male figures is ... the "proffering position": the men sit with legs thrown wide apart, crotch visible, feet pointing outward, often with an arm and casually dangling hand resting comfortably on an open, spread thigh.'[66]

Gendered performances, then, establish the boundaries of what are regarded as 'stable bodily contours'[67] for women and men. These performances produce particular notions of sexed bodies – permeable, penetratable females and impermeable, penetrating males – and notions of what counts as sexual practise linked to these notions of sexed bodies. One is either heterosexually male or female.

Normalized performances of femininity and masculinity produce what counts as sex and sexuality and standardize a notion of heterosexual culture as 'the elemental form of human association, as the very model of intergender relations, as the indivisible basis of all community.'[68] It is little wonder that those who believe in a binary gender frame in which female and male bodies are complementarily heterosexual are upset when a male body performs femininity. By implication, he is permeable. But, if male bodies can be permeable and female bodies can penetrate, it is possible to rethink the assumed continuity from gender to sex, sexual practice, and desire.[69]

Sport Discipline and the Production of Gender and Sexuality

It may be suggested that masculinizing and feminizing practices associated with the body are at the heart of the social construction of masculinity and femininity and that this is precisely why sport matters in the total structure of gender relations.[70]

The number of girls vulnerable to a diagnosis of 'Gender Identity Disorder' has dramatically increased as girls become more assertive and as they engage in the 'rough-and-tumble play' that, 'in psychological terminology, is the hallmark of the male child.'[71] Ruckers, Becky's psychiatrist, thinks, for example, that gender identity disorder can be determined by comparing a child with same-sex, same-aged peers in athletic skills such as throwing a ball and the percentage of baskets made from the free-throw line. As Burke sardonically comments, 'I ... hate to think that a child's diagnosis of mental health ... depend[s] on basketball shots made, or not made, from the free throw line.'[72] That uncoordinated boys and co-ordinated girls are vulnerable to a gender-identity-disorder diagnosis has quite profound implications for ways in which sport programs are administered.

For boys, sport is an important place to try out performances of masculinity since the constitutive skills of most sport are also constitutive of conventional masculinity.[73] Boys who are not interested in sport are as sanctioned as those girls who are. As Whitson writes, '[D]emonstrating the physical and psychological attributes associated with success in athletic contests has now become an important requirement for status in most adolescent and preadolescent male peer groups.'[74] Commenting about the attraction of combative sports for men, Whitson writes that 'body contact sports are now one of the few areas of public life in which force and intimidation are still allowed to triumph, where men who love to hit can still enjoy doing so, and others will celebrate their toughness and their willingness to pay the price.'[75] While Whitson emphasizes that male bodies are masculinized in sport, it is also important to notice that sport is a site in which what counts as a male body is reinforced through repetition of movements that suggest impermeability, forcefulness, and strength.

If one takes seriously the assumptions that link gender, sex, sexual desire, and sexual practice, sport for girls has the potential to increase 'gender deviance.'[76] Conventional notions of masculinity and femininity and of male and female bodies are troubled when girls and women are present in sport. Even 'feminine' sports such as figure skating and synchronized swimming accommodate female bodies uneasily. Performance of skills constitutive of both 'femininity' and 'feminine' sports – skills such as grace, ease, and charm – invoke the binary gender frame of femininity and masculinity, but do so tenuously, because strength and speed, even though masked, are necessary for 'feminine' sport as well.

I am looking at photographs by Annie Leibovitz of U.S. Olympic athletes published in *Vanity Fair*.[77] One of the photographs is of a grouping of highly muscular individuals, one of whom is supporting the shoulders and the other the legs of someone in a horizontal position. This person, in turn, is supporting the weight of another who is standing in a crouched position on the stomach and thighs of the person in the horizontal position. When I first looked at this photograph, I thought I was seeing an elaborate pose by bodybuilders. I was only aware that this was a photograph of women when I focused on the fact that the athletes were wearing women's bathing suits. I had to read the caption beside the photograph to realize that the athletes were female synchronized swimmers in an underwater manoeuvre.

The tremendous display of strength represented in this photograph is the necessary prelude to an above-water display of flexibility, grace, and expression. Literally kept under water is the strength, skill, and stamina required to set up this feminine pose. Synchronized swimmers are the quintessential female athlete but, unlike other female athletes, they keep their strength and skill under water, subterranean, hidden. Synchronized swimming requires this subterfuge and, therefore, is a metaphor for femininity itself.

The fear of 'gender deviance' has meant that female participation in sport has been strictly policed and monitored.[78] In the early part of the twentieth century in North America, medical doctors and female physical educators advised against vigorous exercise and 'unhealthy,' 'unnatural' competition that, they cautioned, would tax female bodies to the point of hysteria, damage female reproductive systems, and contribute to 'mannishness.' Media still portray female athletes as novelties, beauty queens, or 'mannish' freaks, and there is ongoing fear-mongering from media, administrators, coaches, and the sporting public about the '"mannish" athlete and the lesbian threat.'[79] An effect of these measures has been to convey the message that, if women wish to participate in sport, they must do so in ways that are minimally disruptive of sport as a process contributing to a two gender–two sex system, or else be punished.

One of the more striking ways in which sport works to reinforce gender categories is through 'gender verification' or 'sex testing.' Sex testing entails scraping tissue from the inside of the athlete's cheek and then analysing this tissue for X and Y chromatin. Jennifer Hargreaves comments that '"sex testing" ... was introduced in order to prevent males from competing in women's events, and so it also symbolizes the idea of male athletic superiority.'[80] Since strength, skill, and aggression are considered to be masculine performances and these performances solidify notions of maleness, someone who excels at these performances is presumed to be male. Even females in mixed competitions such as equestrian events must undergo sex testing,[81] because sex testing 'is the most potent symbol of the concern to prove that there is an absolute distinction between the sexes.'[82]

In 1966 female athletes were visually inspected to verify their 'femininity' at the European Championships in Track and Field in Budapest, and in 1968 the International Olympic Committee (IOC) instituted mandatory chromosomal testing of women athletes at the Mexico Olympics.[83] The IOC persists with 'sex testing' despite evidence that chromosomes are not neatly packaged as XX or XY and that sex assignment based on chromosomal readings is often related to assumptions about genitalia. Medical doctors have declared individuals to be male who have XX chromosomes ('normal' for females) because of the presence of external genitalia. John Hood-Williams comments that these individuals with XX chromosomes 'were assigned as men, we have to presume ... because of the appearance of external genitalia. But, of course, in some circumstances physicians decide that the external genitalia should be surgically "corrected" since they do not match the chromosomal sex.'[84] Part of the difficulty with attempting to line up chromosomes with genitalia and these, in turn, with an assignment of biological sex is that there are not just two sexes into which all bodies fit. Medical science is aware of the existence of at least five sexes – what Anne Fausto-Sterling refers to as male, intersexed male, true intersexed male, intersexed female, and female.[85] Despite this knowledge, those whose bodies do not match the normal standard for femaleness or maleness are 'normalized' through surgical alteration.

Anti-drug campaigns in high-performance sport are also based on an assumption that sexual dimorphism is a natural fact that steroids undermine. These campaigns have often relied on scare tactics which send the message that by taking steroids, one's sex will be changed.[86] Davis and Delano argue that anti-drug campaigns assume a dichotomization of 'physical gender' that 'conceal[s] the physical realities of many people ... and label[s] such people as ugly, freakish, and disgusting.'[87]

The norm in high-performance sport is masculine and heterosexual. Repetition of sport skills in men's sport materializes notions of a male body as forceful and impermeable and invokes the gendered binary frame – a masculine body as heterosexually complementary to a necessarily absent female body or a female body cheering on the sidelines. Women and 'effeminate' gay men in sport disrupt this masculine, heterosexual norm for athletic bodies. Women do so by undermining an assumption that there is a coherence between gendered performance and sexed bodies. When bodies identified as female perform masculine skills, questions emerge about the presumed softness, passivity, and permeability of female bodies.

A stereotypical gay man in sport calls into question the assumed immutability of conventional masculinity. As Brian Pronger indicates, '[B]eing both athletic and gay presents a seeming contradiction.'[88] For the most part, however, gay men are invisible in sport. Whereas lesbians are assumed to predominate in women's sport, gay men are assumed to be absent. Locker-room talk ensures that everyone understands that gays are outsiders to sport because they are not masculine, more like girls and women, and hence certainly not athletes. Teasing and ridiculing other boys and men about being a 'fag' is the most common way that both athletes and coaches police sexuality in sport.[89]

Recently, figure skating has purportedly become more masculine because many skaters are performing more athletic and less artistic movements and are wearing fewer sequins and more leather. According to some sport journalists, a new 'macho' look has made men's figure skating more interesting.[90] 'Macho,' 'cowboy,' and 'daring dirt-bike look' are coded as heterosexual, even though these images have cultural meaning in gay male culture as well.[91] If we have any doubts about the sexuality of at least some of the skaters, mainstream sport journalists are willing to help us out: '[H]e's on the ice at 8 a.m. Two hours later, he's at work. He has skating bills and a family to look after, a one-year-old and a seven-year-old stepdaughter.'[92]

Lesbians in sport are perhaps less disruptive of an assumed coherence among sex, gender, and sexual practice to the extent that performances by lesbians in sport match stereotypical notions of the masculine lesbian. Yet there is an ongoing policing of lesbianism in sport that affects all women. As Cahn indicates, '[W]omen can compete, even excel, in sports as long as they demonstrate that they are sexually interested in and accessible to men.'[93] Those who do not make their heterosexuality apparent are targets of anti-lesbian harassment. An extreme, but common, example is Rene Portland, who as coach of the Pennsylvania State women's basketball team dismissed players when she uncovered that they were lesbians.[94] 'Portland's antilesbian bias even translated into fear for straight players. "Rene told us when we came on the team that she didn't go for the lesbian life-style, that she didn't want it on her team – wouldn't tolerate it ... I'm not a lesbian, but when I played for her, I was afraid she might think I was and take away my scholarship. I started changing the way I dressed, started going out with a guy I didn't like – just to stay on the team. It meant my academic career, that scholarship."'[95]

Female athletes who worry about their femininity and sexuality find a number of ways to work out the incongruity between their female bodies and their 'masculine' performances. I recall happily quoting my grade-eleven basketball coach that 'we play like boys on the court and behave like ladies off the court.' While many women stay away from sport altogether for fear of the lesbian label, others perform a hyper-femininity when not training or competing. Female athletes often attempt to reconcile their beliefs about female embodiment and sexuality with the 'masculine' gestures and movements they perform in competition by an exaggeration of feminine comportment, dress, and make-up, particularly immediately after competition.

Despite the fact that discourses and technologies of sport discipline reinforce conventional sexuality, sport is often a site of identity formation for lesbians and gay men. Many men, including gay men, are attracted to sport as a way to prove their maleness and, for some, to divert attention from their homosexuality. Olympian Tom Waddell, who was also the founder of the Gay Games, indicated that he became involved in sport because 'I wanted to be viewed as a male ... I wanted the male, macho image of an athlete.'[96]

As Cahn indicates, 'the paradox of women's sport history' is that simultaneous with homophobic fear of the mannish lesbian in sport, there are lesbians in sport who struggle 'to create new ways of being female in a society profoundly afraid of women's sexual autonomy and collective power.'[97] Sport provides a context within which women who are unsure about or coming to terms with their sexual identity can 'explore different social and sexual possibilities.'[98] Indeed, even committed heterosexual women experience in sport what it is like to cross-dress and perform conventional masculine skills.

Discourses and Technologies of Race

I have argued that what counts as a sexed body is interpreted through cultural lenses. The same can be said about what counts as embodiment for other identity categories. In a convincing essay, 'The Suit and the Photograph,' John Berger argues, for example, that there is a recognizable working-class embodiment produced by physical work.[99] Berger writes that even though there are many variations and exceptions, it is possible to note a 'characteristic physical rhythm which most peasants, both women and men, acquire' that is directly related to the amount of work that is performed each day.[100] When peasants or working-class people wear clothes that were designed for those who are sedentary, they are, says Berger, 'condemned ... within the system of those standards, to being always, and recognizably to the classes above them, second-rate, clumsy, uncouth, defensive.'[101]

Even though both sex and gender are cultural, a distinction between sex as biological and gender as cultural *has* been helpful as a way to undermine arguments that behaviour is biological. Unfortunately, there has not been comparable differentiation in understanding race and, consequently, race is still understood by many as entirely biological. Marilyn Frye goes some way in exposing the social underpinnings of race by distinguishing between what she calls being 'whitely' and having white skin.[102] Frye writes: '[B]eing whitely (like being masculine) I conceive as a deeply ingrained way of being in the world. Following the analogy with masculinity, I assume that the connection between whiteliness and light-colored skin is a *contingent* connection: this character could be manifested by persons who are *not* "white"; it can be absent in persons who *are*.'[103]

In distinguishing 'whiteliness' as behaviour from white skin as a feature of bodies, Frye does not consider, however, that what counts as characteristics of whiteness are interpreted through and solidified by performances of 'whiteness.' I want to propose that, just as performances of masculinity solidify what counts as a male body, 'whitely' performances solidify the notion of what counts as a white body. This is not a denial of the physicality or materiality of skin colour and other features. Rather, it is to contend that, like sexed bodies, what counts as the boundaries or limits of a 'raced' body is constructed within expectations of what these bodies do or should perform.

Variations in skin colour and facial features have been reduced to three categories – that is, into three races. Anthropologist Alan Goodman comments that 'race as a way of organizing [what we know about variation] is incredibly simplified and bastardized ... There is no organizing principle by which you could put 5 billion people into so few categories in a way that would tell you anything important about humankind's diversity.'[104] Yet cultural performances of 'raced' behaviour continue to solidify the notion that human variation in skin colour and facial features can be reduced to three categories.

Culturally dominant notions of white bodies are, in part, the consequence of 'whitely' bodily comportment that operates within confined spatial constraints. The 'whitely' comportment of the Aryan Nazi soldier is the epitome of 'whitely' gesture and movement, designed to represent 'whiteness' as clean, pure, contained, orderly, controlled, restrained, and disciplined.[105] Likewise, culturally acquired 'blackly'[106] gestures, comportment, and movement produce or materialize what is perceived to be the physical dimensions of a black body. The boundaries or limits of these gestures, comportment, and movement are often expansive and solidify the bodily contours of blackness as 'strong, athletic' or as 'potent ... savage, animal.'[107] In this culture, 'contained, orderly, restrained, disciplined' people are those in positions of authority – those who judge or help others[108] – and 'strong,' 'potent' people are often athletes.

Whiteliness or blackliness have much different meanings on male or female bodies and, as a result, materialize what counts as whiteness and blackness in much different ways. Black males are often thought by whites to have superior athletic abilities, abilities also linked to masculinity. Black males may take up this stereotype and cultivate what Richard Majors calls the 'cool pose'[109] – 'a construction of unique, expressive, and conspicuous styles of demeanor, speech, gesture, clothing, hairstyle, walk, stance, and handshake ... as a means to show the dominant culture (and the black male's peers) that the black male is strong and proud and can survive.'[110] These performances are solidified into a bodily 'hyper masculinity' and 'hyper(hetero)sexuality in contrast to the norm of conventional white masculinity.

In a racist culture, light skin defines a male as rational and a female as beautiful. A performance of conventional femininity by a dark-skinned female is, then, at odds with conventional beauty. Because 'dark skin is stereotypically coded ... as masculine,'[111] someone who is dark-skinned is never quite able to perform conventional femininity even with cosmetic assistance. Moreover, the history of black women in North America as 'slaves, tenant farmers, domestics, and wageworkers disqualifie[s] them from standards of femininity defined around the frail or inactive female body.[112] The racist association of masculinity with dark skin in this culture makes it possible, then, to more readily associate sport with black womanhood than with white womanhood. As Susan Cahn writes, 'The assertion that sport made women physically unattractive and sexually unappealing found its corollary in views of black women as less attractive and desirable than white women. The correspondence between stereotyped depictions of black womanhood and athletic females was nearly exact, and thus doubly resonant in the case of African American women athletes.'[113]

Nevertheless, most black women's lives defy and exceed the stereotypes. A study by Mimi Nichter indicates, for example, that there is 'growing evidence that black and white girls view their bodies in dramatically different ways.'[114] Said one black girl, '[I]n our culture, women are the power. Often the woman is the sole parent, who holds down two jobs, takes care of the house, raises the children, works in the church. And power means, being large in every way. Big is healthy, strong.'[115]

Sport Discipline and the Production of Race

There right in front of the student union, was a statute entitled *The Student Body*. It was a collection of cast bronze figures, slightly smaller than life-size. One was of an apparently white, Mr. Chips-style figure with a satchel of books on his back, pursuing his way. Another was of a young woman of ambiguous racial cast, white or maybe Asian, carrying a violin and some books and earnestly pursuing her way. A third figure was of a young white woman struggling with a load of books stretching from below her waist up to her chin ... In the center of this arrangement was a depiction of an obviously black young man. He was dressed in gym shorts and balanced a basketball on one finger. The last figure was of a solemn-faced young black woman; she walked along, a solitary book balanced on her head.[116]

I have argued that what counts as identifiable features of a white or black body are established through bodily comportment – white as orderly and contained; black as powerful and strong – as well as through expectations of what 'roles' these bodies can rightfully assume in a culture. Not only is whiteness associated with certain qualities such as 'personal drive, responsibility, integrity, and success,'[117] when someone who is black displays these qualities his or her blackness may be overlooked. In 'The Facts of Michael Jordan's Blackness,' David Andrews shows how Chicago Bulls superstar Michael Jordan's blackness fades when Jordan is represented as successful and responsible. Instead of breaking down the stereotype of 'the responsible white' and 'the irresponsible Black,' Michael Jordan is represented *as* white because, in this culture, to be responsible and a success 'mean[s] *white.*'[118]

High-performance sport contributes to the demarcation of racial identities by reinforcing another stereotype: white athletes are successful in sport because of their intelligence and hard work and black athletes succeed because of their 'natural' athleticism. The publication of *The Bell Curve: Intelligence and Class Structure in American Life*[119] has kept this racist myth alive by claiming to have found a genetically based deficiency in blacks on IQ tests. The authors argue that blacks should become more involved in activities that will develop pride in black communities instead of receiving special educational opportunities. As C. Roger Rees comments, 'In other words, to paraphrase Marie Antoinette, "Let them play basketball."'[120]

When blacks do play basketball and dominate in the sport, this dominance is taken as evidence for genetic differences between blacks and whites. Black athletes are caught in a double bind. When exhibiting superb skill in sport, they reinforce the stereotype of blacks as 'naturally' stronger and consumed by their physicality. Their accomplishments in sport are not attributed to skill and knowledge.[121] Yet, if blacks do not engage in sport, they are cut off from one of the few means available for at least some black people in North America to gain public recognition and, in the case of black men, financial reward for their abilities. For many black males, sport is one of the few contexts within which they can perform conventional masculinity. As Majors comments, '[M]any black males have accepted the definitions, standards, and norms of dominant social definitions of masculinity ... but access to the legitimate means to achieve these goals has been largely denied [them].'[122]

In an article written almost ten years ago, Susan Birrell critiqued the way in which sport sociologists take up racial relations in sport. She argued that, by focusing on black male athletes, sport sociologists equate '"race" ... with Black, obscuring other racial identities.'[123] It should also be emphasized that, when 'race' is equated with black, there need not be any attempt to understand the ways in which sport contributes to the construction of whiteness. For many 'white' scholars, it is still the case that to be concerned with 'race' is to study people of colour (just as, for some, to be concerned about gender is to study women). As Catherine Hall comments, '[I]t is only relatively recently that white people have begun to address explicitly the historical specificity of their own "racial" and ethnic identities, to explore the ways in which whiteness has been constructed as a vital element in power relations, to specify the gendered nature of that whiteness and the inadequacy of a homogeneous notion of white.'[124]

The problematic of 'race' in sport requires much more than providing equal time for experiences of other racial identities, although this may be a necessary first step. Also required is a tracing of the mechanisms or technologies of sport that contribute to the reification of racial boundaries. These will be studies of 'racial relations,' but they will likely not focus on ways in which those of different 'races' get along with each other. Rather, these 'racial relations studies' will seek to describe and reveal processes by which experiences are differentially constructed in sport according to assumptions about race and, as important, how these differences, in turn, serve to demarcate the cultural boundaries of whiteness as 'the standard.'

A good illustration of how racial categories can become reified even as there is an attempt to expose 'the myth of race' is John Hoberman's *Darwin's Athletes: How Sport Has Damaged Black America and Preserved the Myth of Race*. Hoberman ably shows the racist implications of athleticizing black identity, but he also argues that racial categories can be scientifically significant categories, in part 'because they are useful in organizing data.'[125] This begs the question about why one would organize data in this way in

the first place. It also misses the point that, by starting with these categories, a researcher must predetermine or 'operationalize' what characteristics make up the categories. Hoberman states, for example, that 'separate
hemoglobin norms for whites and blacks are widely accepted, if still controversial.'[126] But 'What Color is Black?'[127] At what shade of black would
someone no longer be considered to be black for the purposes of measur-
ing hemoglobin? Setting categories and stipulating at least some of the
characteristics of these categories in advance limits what can be learned
about variations in hemoglobin or, for example, sport skills across human
beings.

Normalization and Athletes with Disabilities

Nowhere is the problematic of 'norming the non-standard' more evident
than when experts intervene to change individuals with impairments so
that they can be integrated into day-to-day activities with those who are
not impaired. This integration or 'norming' takes many different forms:
from elaborate devices designed to make it possible for paraplegics to
walk to interventions by experts to 'norm' speech, hearing, or movement
patterns. Normalization requires that individuals change so that their
abilities and interests match the social context within which they must
live. When they do not match, disability is created or constructed by the
social context. In order to draw out what is meant by the social construction of disability, I first turn to the United Nations (1983) definitions of
impairment, disability, and handicap.

> *Impairment*: Any loss or *abnormality* of psychological, physiological, or ana-
> tomical structure or function. *Disability*: Any restriction or lack (resulting
> from impairment) of ability to perform an activity in the manner or within
> the range considered *normal* for a human being. *Handicap*: A disadvantage
> for a given individual, resulting from impairment or disability, that limits or
> prevents the fulfillment of a role that is *normal*, depending on age, sex,
> social, and cultural factors, for that individual.
>
> Handicap is therefore a function of the relationship between disabled
> persons and their environment. It occurs when they encounter cultural,
> physical, or social barriers which prevent their access to the various systems
> of society that are available to other citizens. Thus handicap is the loss or

limitation of opportunities to take part in the life of the community on an equal level with others.[128]

While these distinctions have some usefulness, particularly because they make possible the inclusion of debilitating chronic illnesses,[129] I am inclined to agree with activists from the disability movement who distinguish between impairment and disability, but see no need to distinguish further between disability and handicap. As Oliver indicates, to be impaired is to lack 'part of or all of a limb, or have a defective limb, organ or mechanism of the body ... [whereas] disability [i]s the disadvantage or restriction of activity caused by a contemporary social organization which takes little or no account of people who have physical impairments.'[130] Susan Wendell argues that, by defining impairment and disability in physical terms and handicap in cultural, physical, and social terms, the U.N. document makes an arbitrary distinction between the physical and social aspects of disability. Wendell reminds us that 'not only the "normal" roles for one's age, sex, society, and culture, but also "normal" structure and function and "normal" ability to perform an activity, depend on the society in which the standards of normality are generated.'[131] Such factors as 'social expectations, the state of technology and its availability to people in that condition, the educational system, architecture, attitudes toward physical appearance, and the pace of life' affect the point at which variation from the norm becomes a disability.[132]

How and whether one is disabled or enabled by a social context depends on 'the relationship of a physical impairment and the political, social, even spatial environment that places that impairment in a matrix of meanings and significations.'[133] Indeed, McDermott and Varenne indicate, cultures 'actively organize ways for persons to be disabled.'[134] 'The difficulties that people in wheelchairs (or city shoppers with carts) face with curbs and stairs tell us little about the physical conditions requiring wheelchairs or carts,' according to McDermott and Varenne, 'but a great deal about the rigid institutionalization of particular ways of handling gravity and boundaries between street and sidewalk as different zones of social interaction.'[135]

When some are at a disadvantage as a result of the way in which a social context is organized, disability is an *effect* of the social context or, in other words, disability is socially constructed. Martha's Vineyard in the eighteenth and nineteenth centuries is a striking example of an absence of disability in a community, even though there were a number of people who had a physical impairment. What was unusual about this community was not only that many people in the community were deaf, but also that almost everyone in the community signed.[136] Surviving members of the community could not always remember who had been deaf because almost everyone in Martha's Vineyard used sign language, including hearing people with other hearing people.[137] This is an example of how in some situations it may be possible to 'eliminate the category of the disabled altogether, and simply talk about individuals' physical abilities in their social context.'[138]

The context of wheelchair basketball, for example, is not disabling for those who can perform the skills of wheelchair basketball and these participants are not disabled. Only when measured against ability standards not applicable to wheelchair participants, but in relation to which they may be deficient, does it make sense to refer to the participants in these activities as disabled. Someone in a wheelchair is not disabled by wheelchair basketball if that person has acquired skills of the activity, but he or she *is* disabled by a game of basketball that does not accommodate wheelchairs. A physical activity for people with disabilities distinguishes an activity for people who are disabled by the larger culture but who are not disabled within these physical-activity contexts. Likewise, someone attempting to run and jump in a wheelchair basketball game would not be enabled. I am reluctant, however, to call this person 'disabled.' In almost every other context aside from wheelchair basketball, the person who can run and jump is enabled.

When measured against high-performance athletes, those who have not been immersed in sport discipline have very little ability. Almost everyone is rendered 'abnormal' in relation to the standards of national, international, or professional sport. On the other hand, if measured in relation to an average performance for a population, the rarified skills of high-performance athletes are 'abnormal.' Like other contexts that rely on establishing who has the most ability, sport is enabling for some and not others. Target height and size, playing-surface size, and equipment size and shape all affect who will be enabled as a performer. Someone who is very short is not enabled by a game like basketball because of the height of the vertical target. Someone who is very tall is not enabled by gymnastics because of the requirement that a performer lift and manipulate the weight of his or her own body. Moreover, sport takes place in a social context in which practice facilities, instruction, technological performance enhancers, and competitive opportunities are not uniformly available. Those with greater access to these social conditions are enabled to compete, while those with less access are not.

Technological Intervention and Disruption of 'the Natural'

In order to alter those who are 'abnormal' so that they are as close to 'the normal' population as possible, interventionist technologies are developed by disciplines to make it possible for individuals to 'adjust' to their environment.[139] By technological intervention I simply mean an organized, systematic, expert application of techniques, mechanisms, or practices designed to normalize or standardize performance or behaviour.

Interventionist technologies such as biomechanical adjustments, repetitive skill exercises, and resistance training are necessary if skill in physical activity is to improve to meet the standards for the activity. These interventions are commonly regarded as 'natural' performance enhancers and those who use them are regarded as 'natural' participants, in contrast to 'unnatural' technological interventions such as performance-enhancing drugs and the 'unnatural' participants who use them. This contrast between 'natural' and 'unnatural' technologies and participants is also used to distinguish between participants with disabilities and able-bodied participants. When technologies are utilized by persons with disabilities to 'adjust' to participation in 'normal' physical activity, the use of these technologies constructs this person as 'unnatural' in contrast to a 'natural' able-bodied participant, even though both able-bodied and disabled participants utilize technologies in order to participate.

When it is assumed that some technologies like resistance training are 'natural,' that other technologies like wheelchairs and prostheses are 'unnatural,' and still others, like steroids, are unethical *because* 'unnatural,' this category confusion makes it possible to argue that those who use 'unnatural' technologies should not participate with or compete against those who only utilize 'natural' technologies. In competitive sport this requires that 'natural' able-bodied athletes be separated from 'unnatural' athletes with disabilities. When, however, it is recognized that all participants rely on technological intervention as they aim to meet or surpass the standards or norms for their activities, not only is the dichotomy between the 'natural' able-bodied participant and the 'unnatural' disabled participant called into question, there is potential to disrupt the specious link that is sometimes made between technological intervention and ethical impropriety. Some technologies such as performance-enhancing drugs are arguably ethically problematic, but linking technology to 'the unnatural' and then to the unethical not only commits the 'naturalistic fallacy,' which is to 'take disputed values and make them seem innate, essential, eternal, nonnegotiable,'[140] it undermines physical activity for people with disabilities who rely on technology.

It is often necessary to categorize participants in order to achieve fair competition, but separation of disabled and able-bodied participants is not legitimate when this separation is based on assumptions about 'natural' abilities. Until the late 1970s, athletes with disabilities competed in their disability classification based on medical diagnosis of potential.[141] For the most part athletes are now grouped according to a functional classification system that assesses ability related to strength, range of motion, motor coordination, and balance.[142] Functional classification makes possible integrated competitions in which athletes are assessed and compete across disability classifications.

Competition between those with, say, amputations and those with cerebral palsy does not deny the physicality of differences between them. What these competitions avoid is the assumption that it is possible to know in advance what each individual can do. Claims to be able to assess potential performance based on impairment are claims to be able to distinguish the natural from the social. There is, of course, a limit on what any human body can do. We can neither fly nor stay underwater for long periods of unassisted time and, while there surely are limits on how fast, how high, and how far human beings can go, it is not clear what these limits are for male or female athletes with or without disabilities. Yet, as we have seen, when female athletes surpass the predictions or expectations for performance, this has not called into question the predictions of potential. Rather, it has called into question their status as female. Female athletes who have surpassed predictions of potential have been considered to be genetically suspect – they have been considered to be men.[143]

Some worry that an emphasis on ability rather than on disability will take attention away from adaptation/modification of activities and make it more likely that the more severely impaired will be eliminated from athletic competition.[144] Hans Lindstrom comments that, 'just as a person with a short stature would not choose high jumping or basketball for his sport [and a person with fine motor coordination would not choose a sport that tests minimal fine motor coordination], so a disabled person should not choose a sport that does not suit his or her functional ability.'[145] Lindstrom argues that there should not be swimming events in the International Games for the Disabled that permit the use of floating devices or allow a coach to swim beside the competitor.[146] My argument, by contrast, is that all types of participation should be enabled. Rather than ruling out those who require floating devices or a coach's assistance, those who don't require these techniques should be ruled out of this particular competition.

Interestingly, those who argue for functional classification within sport for disabled athletes do not question separate men's and women's competitions. Lindstrom argues, for example, that muscle mass is a reason to separate men and women in competition.[147] This not only assumes that muscle mass equates with athletic ability, it takes for granted that men 'naturally' have muscle mass and that women cannot acquire muscle mass, and, of course, it undermines an argument for functional classification in sport for people with disabilities. That a move to a functional system of classification has not broken down a male-female division in sport for people with disabilities is an indication that notions of 'natural' male and female abilities have a very strong hold.

Recognizing that all athletes are cyborgs produced by technology helps to dismantle the ability-disability binary and makes it possible to recognize other ways in which athletes are hybrids – 'uneasy coalition[s]' of identities.[148] As Donna Haraway writes, '[C]yborgs ... make very problematic the statuses of man or woman, human, artefact, member of a race, individual entity, or body.'[149] If technology improves ability, and ability is what is important in high-performance competitions, does one need to notice a cyborg's impairment, genitalia, skin colour, or sexual practices? What part of a cyborg is gendered, light-skinned, or heterosexual, for example? Stating it this way underlines the absurdity of limiting chances for those who want to test ability.[150] Moreover, it highlights the mutability of standards or norms of ability, whether these are attached to gender, sexuality, race, class or, indeed, sport performance.

Sport as the preserve of white, privileged men no longer has the currency at the millennium that it did with the emergence of modern sport in England in the eighteenth and nineteenth centuries. Sport discipline at the millennium is still relentless in its preparation of skilled athletes, but the diversity and hybridity of athletes make it impossible for modern sport to produce homogeneous athletes. Demands from other parts of an athlete's identity do not always coincide with demands from high-performance sport, resulting in 'necessary failures.'[151] These failures open up gaps in which it is possible for athletes to make some decisions about how they will participate in high-performance sport. In the final chapter I situate a new sport ethics within these gaps. Before doing that, in the next chapter I look at how demands of sport discipline produce ethical issues and how the scholarly field of sport ethics has been produced to contend with these issues. It is to these tasks that I now turn.

CHAPTER FOUR

Ethical Issues and the Scholarly Field of Sport Ethics

Conflicts between people are produced whenever constraints conflict with the interests of those who are constrained. Because athletes and coaches bring different backgrounds and interests to high-performance sport, there is no uniform response to ethical conflicts or issues produced by the constraints of sport discipline. Hybrid participants bring hybrid responses to ethical issues and to interactions with team-mates and opponents. Even so, it would be unusual to find an adult athlete engaged in high-performance sport who fundamentally disagreed with the values of sport discipline. A high-performance athlete not only embodies the skills of a particular sport, he or she embodies the values that underpin the discipline and make these skills possible. Embodiment of what count as values and skills in a particular context or culture, like the embodiment of athletic values and skills, is a consequence of attention to and immersion in these values and skills.[1] As Iris Murdoch argues, what someone gives regular attention to builds up structures of value around that person, so that 'by the time the moment of choice has arrived the quality of attention has possibly determined the nature of the act.'[2]

Regular attention to ethical values and regular repetition of what counts as an ethical response produces ethically skilled people. Like the feminine woman who internalizes and self-polices the values of conventional femininity, an ethical person does not need to be watched to do the 'right' thing nor does he or she need to refer to some external standard as a prompt.[3] To desire to respond to ethical predicaments is to internalize an ethical panopticon. Like an automatic response by an athlete to a competitive situation, an automatic response to what is perceived as an ethical situation is a disciplined response. It is an indication of skill and, for those who value the discipline, it is commendable. Having to stop to consider what a response should be or having to be externally monitored in order to respond is an indication of less skill and is less commendable.

Yet, it is also the case that someone who automatically responds conforms to the standards of the discipline. Ethical skill, then, may be less about responsibility, fairness, or 'caring' than about embodied conformity to standards. One might ask, for example, whether a desire to be on time so as not to keep someone waiting is an indication of responsibility or whether to be responsible in this instance is to conform to a standard that supports a particular way of constructing relationships in relation to time. Is one a dupe when one is on time so as not to keep others waiting? How one answers this question depends, in large part, on whether one values these standards. For some, embodying a responsibility to be on time so that others don't wait is an ethically good conformity.

Unlike Foucault, who did not explore the legitimacy of constraints,[4] I am interested both in how the constraints of sport discipline produce ethical conflicts for participants and in the legitimacy of these constraints. I address ethical issues of violence and cheating produced by the demands of sport discipline, but I am also interested in constraints that limit the effects of diversity on teams by advocating an unproblematized rhetoric about communication and trust.

Ethical Issues as Effects of Sport Discipline

In a scathing critique of what he sees as the hypocrisy of sport technologists, scientists, and ethicists, Eugen König argues that doping is perfectly consistent with other technologies that push human limits of performance but that are included as part of 'pure,' 'natural,' and 'authentic' sport because they are not proscribed by the rules. König insists that 'the compulsory and unlimited exploitation of oneself and others is a constituent factor of sport itself.'[5] Doping exposes sport as an enterprise that is inherently exploitative. '[I]f doping is understood as an expression, as a factual realization of a certain form of conscience, as instrumentalized knowledge of how to achieve maximization, then the related structure of sport and doping becomes most obvious. What both have in common is a certain type of knowledge which – as its basic feature – never leaves anything in its actual state, or more precisely, which preserves itself by permanent modifications on an increasingly higher level ... [O]ne of the most advanced aids in sports which corresponds to the most modern level of technology is just what is broadly understood as doping.'[6]

Sport ethicists have tended not to notice the dilemmas that commitment to high-performance sport presents for athletes. Instead, the focus has been on the logic of rules, with the implication that behaviour will change if participants are helped to understand that, when they break proscriptive rules of a sport, they are engaged in practices that are illogical. Pearson puts the argument about rules this way: 'A variety of elegant arguments can be produced to indict the deliberate foul. It violates the ludic spirit, it treats the process of playing as mere instrument in the pursuit of the win and it reflects a view of one's competitor as both enemy and object rather than a colleague in a noble contest. All of these pleas, however, fall short of the ultimate and most damaging testimony; deliberate betrayal of the rules destroys the vital frame of agreement which makes sport possible.'[7]

Sport ethicists argue that deliberate rule breakage undermines the constitutive *logic* of a game: 'If the rules are broken the original end becomes impossible of attainment, since one cannot (really) play the game unless one obeys the rules of the game.'[8] High-performance coaches and athletes, on the other hand, are often more compelled by the constitutive *demands* of sport discipline that athletes 'push on until the limits of human performance capacity are reached.'[9] Since, in competitive sport, who wins the contest often indicates who has been most willing to push the limits, a desire to achieve the constitutive demands of sport very often overrides the constitutive logic of rules. Indeed, in order to achieve the constitutive demands of high-performance sport, participants often must break rules. This includes such infractions as using the hands in soccer or holding opponents in football and it includes breaking proscriptions against violence and performance enhancers like steroids and blood doping.

When opponents realize that cheating or violence is an option for everyone as a means to win games, a genuine paradox or dilemma arises for athletes.[10] This paradox, called the prisoners' dilemma after the anecdote used to describe it in mathematical game theory, has the following dimensions. Two prisoners are charged with the same crime of which they will be convicted only if one of them confesses. The prisoners are told that, if they both confess to the crime, they will both receive five years in jail. If neither confesses, some trumped-up evidence will put them both in jail for three years. If one confesses while the other does not, the one who confesses will receive one year in jail and the who does not confess will receive ten years in jail.

The best outcome, of course, is to spend one year in jail, but this will only occur if one prisoner can be trapped into not confessing when the other is confessing. When this happens, the prisoner who doesn't confess will receive the worst outcome, which is to spend ten years in jail. The worst outcome for each prisoner if they both confess is to spend five years in jail. The best outcome for both is to spend three years in jail, but this can only happen if neither confesses. Since each prisoner attempts to create the best individual outcome, each confesses to the crime and each receives five years in jail. The dilemma is that by attempting to create the best possible outcome for oneself, each is left with an outcome that is not the best for either. Each prisoner knows that the other is attempting to create the best possible self-interested outcome and each chooses to confess for fear that the other will confess. Neither is in a position to cooperate when there is no way of knowing if the other person will cooperate.

One does not need to look far to see instances of prisoner's dilemma–type situations in high-performance sport. When the desire for winning overrides a desire for fairness or care for physical well-being, athletes are likely to become trapped in the prisoner's dilemma. In the case of taking steroids, for example, an athlete may feel that opponents cannot be trusted to refrain from taking steroids and so he or she may feel compelled to take them for fear of being less competitive. Paradoxically, this may place athletes in a far worse situation than they would be in if no participants took steroids. By taking steroids, an athlete risks damage to his or her health and the level of distrust is elevated. Meanwhile, those who attempt to win the contest within the rules become less and less competitive.

I agree with König that ethical issues such as doping are produced by the demands of high-performance sport, which entangle athletes in 'prisoner's dilemmas.' But, because an athlete's interests and desires are not wholly framed by sport discipline, there is no guarantee that an athlete will become entangled. The demands of high-performance sport do not foreclose on what an athlete will do. It is not inevitable that high-performance athletes will break rules or resort to violence in order to push limits of performance. The probability is high only when the desires produced by sport discipline override desires athletes have to be fair. Sport discipline is less likely to consume an athlete the more varied an athlete's experiences in dealing with conflict outside sport and, as we shall see in the next chapter, with opportunities to question demands of high-performance sport that would 'normalize' cheating and violence.

The Imperative of Teamwork

A team is a site of intense interaction among athletes as they attempt to acquire skills together. Teams are often represented as a type of community or a family, whose members are bonded together to achieve the goal of winning games. Team goals are usually stipulated in terms of quantifiable performance outcomes, while means to achieve these goals are understood in relation to unquantifiable notions of teamwork,[11] team cohesiveness,[12] or team spirit[13] and other social factors such as communication, collaboration, and trust.[14] For example, Syer indicates that team spirit is 'the joy of working toward a shared objective with a group of which I am glad to be a part'[15] and Larson and LaFasto write that 'teamwork succeeds most dramatically when team members are enthusiastically unified in pursuit of a common objective rather than individual agendas.'[16]

Collaboration and achievement of common goals are thought to be possible if there is open communication in which participants are encouraged to not only share their experiences,[17] but to disclose and share information openly, especially negative information.[18] Trust, in particular, is considered to improve collaboration and promote efficient communication and coordination.[19] 'Trust allows team members to stay problem-focused. The absence of trust diverts the mental concentration and energy of a team away from its performance objective and onto other issues. The team becomes politicized. Communication becomes guarded and distorted ... Conversely, when trust is present, a collaborative climate is more readily fostered – allowing team members to stay focused on their common problem or goal.'[20] Schellenberger argues that team goals are more easily achieved if team-mates are friends and, on the basis of this assumption, he argues that coaches should attempt to encourage athletes to be friends outside practice sessions and competitions.[21]

The discourse of a team as family or community and team members as friends is familiar even while, as Michael Messner points out, 'individuals on teams are constantly competing against each other – first for a place on the team, then for playing time, recognition, and "star" status, and eventually, just to stay on the team.'[22] While very real antagonisms among team-mates are publicly hidden by the rhetoric of 'team' and often not properly dealt with within the team context for fear that the team will be exposed as dysfunctional, especially to themselves, my interest here is in exploring ethical implications of a constraint on athletes and coaches that I call the imperative of teamwork.

The imperative of teamwork has not been a site for ethical consideration by sport ethicists. This is in part because there *is* much that is valuable about a pursuit that requires people to subsume their interests as they strive to achieve something that is of collective value to them. It is my contention, however, that the imperative of teamwork is ethically problematic when the effect is to overlook differences among athletes and coaches and, in particular, those differences that may constitute them as outsiders or deviants. Open communication and trust are often options only for those athletes and coaches whose views are already valued and who have no reason to distrust coaches and team-mates. In order to show why this is so, I deconstruct what is at stake in calls for teamwork, collaboration, open communication, and trust.

Deconstruction makes apparent that a concept always has a '*beyond* to it, precisely by virtue of what it excludes.'[23] Drucilla Cornell has renamed deconstruction the 'philosophy of the limit' to refer to a process that attempts to locate what is excluded from a text by 'refocuss[ing] attention on the *limits* constraining philosophical understanding.'[24] As Judith Butler asserts, '[T]o deconstruct is ... to call into question and, perhaps more importantly, to open up a term [or text] ... to a reusage or redeployment that previously has not been authorized.'[25]

Are there limits to a call for teamwork in which athletes collaborate on common goals through open communication and trust? An assumption that teamwork will be enhanced through open communication in a context of trust depends upon not noticing that there may be some 'open communication' or 'negative' disclosure that is outside or beyond what is allowable if team cohesiveness is to be retained. There is a limit to rhetoric about open communication and trust when some athletes or coaches are unable to trust that they will not be dismissed from a team or otherwise harmed if some aspect of what is important to them is openly disclosed.

Teamwork, with its rhetoric of communication and trust, can only be sustained when there are restrictions on what can be communicated and on information with which athletes and coaches can be entrusted. There are only certain shared experiences that most teams are able to entertain if they are to retain a sense of cohesiveness. As an obvious example, there is still an imperative on most teams for gay and lesbians to remain silent about their sexuality. 'You did everything you could to hang on to your seat, to make the crew, that you would never jeopardize – you wouldn't even tell the coach you had a cold ... because if there's any perceived weakness, they'll put somebody else in the boat. So to hint that I was gay was to kiss rowing goodbye.'[26]

As in other communities and many mainstream families, gays and lesbians can be included only if everyone assumes a 'don't ask, don't tell' policy. If gays and lesbians were to tell their experiences, it would expose the fact that 'success' of the community, family, or team depends on these experiences not being communicated. There is a limit, then, to teamwork because teamwork is achievable by not noticing that some experiences cannot be told and by not recognizing that this silence is what makes possible the rhetoric of 'open communication,' 'trust,' and 'teamwork.' An imperative of teamwork produces ethical conflicts by making it possible for some but not others to communicate and trust. The silence of some athletes and coaches in a context of 'open communication' is no less an ethical issue produced by the demands of high-performance sport than is cheating and violence. In the next section I say more about why trust is complicated when contextualized by power and diversity.

Coach-Athlete Relationships

I am interested in coach-athlete relationships because the imperative of teamwork requires that athletes and coaches trust each other, even though coaches often exercise more power on teams than do athletes. It is important, then, to be clear that trust between a coach and athlete is sometimes morally problematic, but, as important, one must notice that coaches and athletes do often establish relationships in which there is significant affection, goodwill, and 'morally good trust.'[27]

High-performance athletes enter into relationships with coaches in order to benefit from decisions coaches make on their behalf and, once subjected to sport discipline, athletes willingly follow the decisions coaches make on their behalf. Indeed, sport discipline is effective because disciplined athletes are willing to be told what is in their best interests by those who exercise more power. Production of disciplined skill does not require an authoritative exercise of power. It does, however, often require trust. Coaches trust athletes to be serious about performance goals and not to jeopardize these for the sake of other interests that athletes claim to be less important. Athletes trust coaches to be informed and prepared, provide safe environments, and otherwise make it possible for them to attain athletic goals. Athletes trust coaches to help improve athletic skills and, even when athletes are as knowledgable about skill acquisition and/or game strategies, they often require coaches to observe performances and provide feedback or suggest strategies when there are multiple options.

Yet, as Annette Baier notes, moral philosophy has not asked many questions about trust, even though trust is central to relationships 'not only with intimates but with strangers, and even with declared enemies ... We do in fact, wisely or stupidly, virtuously or viciously, show trust in a great variety of forms, and manifest a great variety of versions of trustworthiness, both with intimates and strangers. We trust those we encounter in lonely library stacks to be searching for books, not victims. We sometimes let ourselves fall asleep on trains or planes, trusting neighboring strangers not to take advantage of our defenselessness. We put our bodily safety into the hands of pilots, drivers, doctors, with scarcely any sense of recklessness.'[28]

What little attention moral philosophy has paid to trust as a morally significant factor in relationships has been in relation to the minimal trust implicit in contracts, based on the Hobbesian assumption of 'minimally trusting, minimally trustworthy adults who are equally powerful.'[29] Contracts attempt to make explicit the boundaries of the relationship between conflicting individuals who exercise equal power and, therefore, miss the relationships many of us have – those with people who exercise less or more power of some kind. As Baier argues, when we ignore relationships between unequals, we miss seeing the ways in which trust is often an important characteristic of these relationships.

In all trusting relations, equal or unequal, the person trusting, whether exercising more or less power, is vulnerable to the person trusted.[30] Trust entails an 'accepted vulnerability to another's possible but not expected ill will (or lack of good will) toward one.'[31] We make ourselves vulnerable to others in this way because we need their help. 'Since the things we typically do value include such things as we cannot singlehandedly either create or sustain (our own life, health, reputation, our offspring and their well-being, as well as intrinsically shared goods such as conversation, its written equivalent, theater and other forms of play, chamber music, market exchange, political life, and so on) we must allow many other people to get into positions where they can, if they choose, injure what we care about, since those are the same positions that they must be in order to help us to take care of what we care about.'[32]

An athlete is willing to submit to a coach's decisions in order to have help with what she or he cares about.[33] Baier advises that what is understood by 'caring for' be specified so that an assessment can be made about why certain decisions or actions 'disappoint rather than meet the trust one has in such circumstances.' In some instances athletes trust coaches to leave them alone. It is not a coach's responsibility to ensure athletes' long-term security, for example, or other values distinct from the athletic context. Most often, however, 'the most important things we entrust to others are things which take more than noninterference in order to thrive.'[34] Decisions by a coach on behalf of an athlete occur because there are certain matters concerning an athlete's performance that an athlete cannot affect alone. An athlete permits a coach access to what he or she cares about in the expectation that the coach will help take care of it.

Mutual trust in a coach-athlete relationship is not always an indication of the moral decency of the relationship, however. Baier writes: '[N]ot all things that thrive when there is trust between people, and which matter, are things that should be encouraged to thrive. Exploitation and conspiracy, as much as justice and fellowship, thrive better in an atmosphere of trust. There are immoral as well as moral trust relationships, and trust-busting can be a morally proper goal.'[35]

Not only do coaches often exercise power accrued from knowledge about the particular sport and/or from a vantage point not available to an athlete, they are often able to exercise power to administer resources, including playing time. Exercising power to control playing time and indeed a player's continued involvement on a team makes it possible for a coach to coerce athletes' behaviour.

Even when coaches exercise power coercively, they must also trust athletes; because of this, coaches are also often vulnerable to athletes. Ironically, it is often an exercise of coercive power that serves to maintain a relationship of (morally problematic) trust between coach and athlete. A coach may be able to maintain her or his trust in an athlete by counting on the knowledge that athletes are concerned not to jeopardize playing time or a spot on the team. Coaches trust that athletes won't be so foolish as to test this threat. When athletes realize that coaches trust that athletes are regulated by this threat, there is opportunity to take advantage of trust. If this is skilfully done, a coach will maintain trust in the athlete despite her or his untrustworthiness. As Baier writes: 'Sensible trust could persist, in conditions where truster and trusted suspect each other of willingness to harm the other if they could get away with it, the one by breach of trust, the other by vengeful response to that. The stability of the relationship will depend on the trusted's skill in cover-up activities, or on the truster's evident threat advantage, or a combination of these ... Where the truster relies on his threat advantage to keep the trust relations going, or where the trusted relies on concealment, something is morally rotten in the trust relationship.'[36] While Baier does not refer to Foucault to make this point, it is clear from this example that power is not unidirectional. Both coaches and athletes exercise power that generates or produces the relationship between them.

Since we do trust in asymmetrical power relations, how can athletes and coaches know when the trust they have in each other is morally good? Baier proposes a moral test for trust relationships: the relationship would 'survive awareness by each party ... of *what* the other relies on' in each other 'to ensure their continued trustworthiness or trustingness.'[37] An athlete's trust in a coach is tested if the athlete comes to understand that the coach relies on the athlete's fear of dismissal from the team or reduced playing time or on the athlete's stupidity in 'not realizing her exploitation, or on her servile devotion ... to keep her more or less trustworthy.'[38] A coach's trust in an athlete is tested if the coach comes to realize that the athlete relies on her or his skill in covering up breaches of trust or relies on the coach's assumption that an athlete would do nothing to jeopardize performance. When trust occurs in coach-athlete relationships in these ways – when 'either party relies on qualities in the other which would be weakened by the knowledge that the other relies on them,'[39] trust is morally bad. Morally decent trust between coach and athlete, on the other hand, occurs when each party relies on the other's 'concern for some common good' and where knowledge of what each other relies on does not 'undermine but will more likely strengthen those relied-on features.'[40] If morally good trust is to flourish, it is important that coach and athletes specify the goals held in common and whether the coach may make decisions about these goals.

Coaches and athletes exercise power asymmetrically largely as a result of the places they occupy within institutions. Trust between coaches and athletes will often fail the test of trust because coaches often exercise coercive power to accomplish team and institutional goals and athletes often take advantage of a coach's trust that players will not jeopardize standing on the team. An athlete may find it inappropriate to trust a coach, however, even when that trust passes the test of trust, because of the institutional context in which trust is required.[41] Coaches often have a vested interest in performance outcomes over and above or often instead of the experiential benefits to athletes. If a coach's employment is in jeopardy when performance outcomes are not reached, the trust an athlete may have in an otherwise trustworthy coach may be compromised by factors not controlled by either of them. In such a context, it is often not a simple matter for an athlete to trust a coach to make decisions on his or her behalf.

Morally good trust between a coach and athlete is also no guarantee that athletes will avoid violent and cheating behaviours. Coaches and athletes can satisfy all the criteria for morally good trust between them and share goals that include using measures such as performance-enhancing drugs, extreme training, violence, and excessive dieting to push the boundaries of human performance. Since dieting, extreme training, ingestion of performance-enhancing drugs, and encouragement of violence and cheating can occur in instances of morally good trust, the possibilities are endless for problematic behaviour when neither coach nor athlete are trustworthy. When the former Olympic swimming coach of

Great Britain was sentenced in 1995 to seventeen years in jail for sexual assault on some of his female athletes, reporters for the *Daily Telegraph* commented that the key to the Olympic coach's power 'lay in the trust essential to any successful coach-swimmer relationship ... Later they all told the same story. Swimming was their life. He had the power to drop them from the team and they dared not speak out.'[42] In 1996 the former coach of a Canadian junior hockey team was sentenced to three and a half years for two counts of sexual abuse. The junior hockey coach was reported to have 'stolen trust and ... confidence in adults.'[43]

Adult and perhaps young athletes may be able to withdraw voluntarily from high-performance sport when the demands overwhelm other interests and desires, but this is a very high price to pay when this ends participation as a high-performance athlete. Child athletes almost never get to make decisions about their continued involvement in sport. Children rarely are given the opportunity to specify what their interests are, grant a coach power to make decisions on their behalf, or work out their goals with a coach. When goals are discussed, it is more often a discussion between parents or guardians and coaches. Parents and coaches might establish the conditions of morally good trust between them and the common goal of these adults may be that the child athlete meet the constitutive *demands* of high-performance sport.

The hybrid identity and complex desires that an adult athlete brings to sport discipline make it possible and often likely that the demands of high-performance sport can be disrupted and even rejected when they conflict with other values. This is not as likely to happen in high-performance sport involving children. Child athletes are less likely to have an array of contradictory desires, interests, and values to offset the excessive demands of high-performance sport, merely because they have not lived long enough to be exposed to competing disciplines. For this reason, I believe it to be inappropriate to immerse a child in any activity that consumes his or her time, controls the space in which he or she functions, and restricts movement to rarified skills, thus closing off the gaps in which the child might diversify interests, desires, and values.

Sport Ethics

Questions concerning children's involvement in high-performance sport have not had much attention in sport ethics[44] because sport ethicists, myself included, have been preoccupied with moral obligations in relation to rules. When what makes a practice worthy of ethical consideration is whether it is related to an agreement to comply with rules, some practices are noticed as ethical issues, while others are subsumed under the normal practices of high-performance sport. Drug taking, the 'good' foul, violence, and cheating are prominent ethical issues in sport ethics, while racism, homophobia, and abuses related to interpersonal relationships have not been. Health problems and injuries that are incurred as a result of performing the prescribed rules of boxing, football, hockey, and gymnastics are not easily accommodated in an ethics that focuses on rule breakage.

A sport ethics that is limited to discussions about obligations to keep the rules is itself produced by the demands of sport discipline. Sport ethics exists in its present form because sport ethicists have had an opportunity to provide expert understanding of the implications of issues such as cheating, violence, and drug taking produced by modern sport. If the demands of sport discipline did not produce rule breakage, there would be no need for sport ethicists to make arguments about obligations to follow rules. Sport ethics has been contained within a discussion about rules, and, as a consequence, it is 'a powerless protest against sport.'[45] and 'actually prevents what it pretends to intend.'[46]

For Foucault, a concern for ethics is a concern for how one is constituted as a subject of one's own actions. In the final chapter, I turn to Foucault's ethics to suggest that a new task for sport ethics is to encourage participants to question their involvement in the normalizing technologies of sport discipline. When aspects of the normalizing process are found to be problematic, it may, then, be possible to refuse these problematic aspects and perhaps create something new. It is my contention that spaces are opened up for questioning, refusal, and creation – features of Foucault's ethics and what I call postmodern interventions – when diverse, hybrid athletes are subjected to the constraints of modern sport. As a consequence, it is also my contention that a central role of a new sport ethics must be the promotion and cultivation of diversity and hybridity.

CHAPTER FIVE

Hybrid Athletes and Discipline: Possibilities for a New Sport Ethics

It has been a purpose of this book to document how high-performance athletes and a set of ethical issues are produced by modern sport discipline. As important, however, I have wanted to show that athlete identity, and hence the ways in which athletes may contend with the demands of sport discipline, including the ethical issues it produces, are necessarily confounded by diversity and hybridity.

My purpose in this final chapter is to show that another way of thinking about ethics in sport is produced when discipline is confronted by diversity. I believe that the juxtaposition of diverse, hybrid participants with the homogenizing and normalizing technologies of sport discipline opens up a space for participants to intervene in their relationships with sport discipline. These interventions, informed by Foucault's ethics, include questioning how sport discipline produces identity, refusing those practices with which one cannot agree or comply, and when possible and desirable, creating new ways of understanding and participating in high-performance sport. This new sport ethics is interested in retaining what is valuable about modern sport, including the production of exquisite skill, while exploring where postmodern diversity might take sport.

Foucault's Ethics

Many readers of Foucault believe that, because Foucault theorized resistance within the matrix of disciplinary power, he permitted no escape from the totalizing effects of disciplinary power. Foucault argued that resistances occur wherever there is power. Resistance, like power, is multiple, and it is 'formed right at the point where relations of power are exercised.'[1] Foucault's understanding that resistance occurs in relation to the exercise of power does circumscribe resistance, but it also opens up possibilities for understanding power dynamics in the day-to-day interactions of people, including athletes with their coaches and with each other.[2]

Coaches do, of course, exercise considerably more power than most athletes because they act in the context of institutions that support their decisions. But athletes also exercise power. They do so whenever they perform skills produced by sport discipline. They also exercise power by resisting coaches. This resistance is rarely in the form of a revolution-like ousting of a coach or even very often in the form of refusing a coach's instructions. Resistance occurs in other ways such as discussions with team-mates and friends after practices and games about coaching methods and decisions, gestures behind the coach's back, refusing expectations for training outside formal practice times, and breaking team rules that proscribe drinking or staying up late. Moreover, because individual acts of resistance occur in a network of power, there is the possibility of linking and coordinating individual resistances within this network. Resistances to the controlling effects of national sport organizations and their coaches by some Canadian high-performance athletes, for example, are linked together to produce an association working on behalf of athletes.[3] This association does not exercise nearly the power that administrators, coaches, and bureaucrats do in high-performance sport in Canada, but it has been able to create a discourse that focuses on athletes' concerns by taking up, or utilizing, the category 'high-performance athlete' produced by sport discipline.[4]

It is correct to be concerned, however, that resistance which occurs only in relation to disciplinary power can do little to change the totalizing effects of discipline. Resistance circumscribed by disciplinary power may provide individuals with a sense of agency as they act within a discipline, but it doesn't challenge the discipline itself. Fortunately, this is not all Foucault had to say about resistance, or refusal, as he later called it. In order to understand how Foucault thought disciplines could be challenged, it is necessary to turn to his work on ethics, written after *Discipline and Punish* and *The History of Sexuality, Volume I*: in particular, *The Use of Pleasure* (volume 2 of *The History of Sexuality*) and his essays 'What Is Enlightenment' and 'The Subject and Power.'

Foucault argued that every morality consists of codes of behaviour as well as ways in which individuals subject themselves to these codes. In those moral systems that emphasize the code, 'the ethical subject refers his conduct to a law, or set of laws, to which he must submit at the risk of committing offenses that may make him liable to punishment.'[5] Foucault reserved the term 'ethics' for those moralities that emphasize 'the manner in which one ought to form oneself as an ethical subject acting in reference to the ... code.'[6]

Ethics is concerned with how one might confront the technologies and discourses of a discipline in its construction of identity. Ethics asks questions about 'the events that have led us to constitute ourselves and to recognize ourselves as subjects of what we are doing, thinking, saying'[7] so that 'we [can] refuse what we are.'[8] Rather than conformity to the law or standards, the emphasis here is on the formation of the relationship with the self and on the methods and techniques through which this relationship is worked out.

Foucault outlined four ways in which someone might embrace or reject a code, each of which is related to aspects of the constitution of the self as a moral subject. First, one must ask what part of one's behaviour is concerned with moral conduct. Is one faithful, to use Foucault's example, because of resolve to follow the rule, feelings for one's partner, or the mastery of desires?[9] Second, one must ask about the source of moral obligations. Is the source external or is it a response to some internal desire? Third comes an inquiry about how one can change in order to become an ethical subject. The final inquiry questions what kind of being one aspires to be when one behaves in a moral way.[10] These four questions are directed at moral codes, but they can also be asked about other codes or standards that make up disciplines which constitute the self.

Ethics, then, involves an investigation not only of one's relationship to moral codes but a genealogical tracing of the events that have constituted us. This investigation provides information with which one can either refuse a particular set of codes or standards or refuse a passive acceptance of what is 'given to us as universal, necessary, and obligatory.'[11] Refusing passively to be involved allows one to meet what Foucault believed to be an obligation to face the endless task of reinventing oneself. Exposing the limits of identity through questioning codes and standards, and then refusing to passively engage these codes and standards, makes it possible to push these limits and create new experiences of subjectivity.

Implications for Sport Ethics

Traditional sport ethics has been preoccupied with identifying codes of behaviour for participating in sport, and when concerned at all with individuals' relations to these codes (what Foucault calls ethics), the focus has been on the second of Foucault's questions, What is the source of moral obligation for sport participants? Sport ethics has not been interested in differentiating the reasons why participants may or may not meet obligations. That participants may abide by rules because coerced, to maintain an image as a 'good' competitor, for expedience, or because of a desire to honour a perceived agreement with competitors does not centre in discussions. This lack of attention to motivations participants have for engaging in particular behaviours can, in part, be explained by the assumption that, if participants can be helped to understand the logic of rules – one can't win a game as constituted by its rules unless one plays by the rules – they will act to comply with rules.

There is no work in sport ethics of which I am aware that encourages participants to explore the constitution of themselves as subjects of sport and other disciplines. I am suggesting, therefore, a new role for sport ethics that takes up the features of Foucault's ethics: a pedagogical role that encourages an active and ongoing questioning by participants of the ways in which sport discipline 'normalizes' practices that would otherwise be considered harmful and that produce athletes capable of and willing to engage in these practices. Part of the new role I see for sport ethics is encouraging those committed to high-performance sport to explore and possibly exploit the gaps that occur when they are faced with a clash between their desires and interests as athletes and their desires and interests from elsewhere. By asking questions about the demands of sport discipline, it is possible for athletes to become aware of how they are produced as high-performance athletes and, once aware, to consent then only to those processes that affirm one's values while refusing the others. In those instances in which an athlete refuses, an opportunity is opened to create other ways of understanding high-performance sport and perhaps other ways of participating.

Noticing Disruptions, Questioning and Refusing Discipline

Questioning normalizing processes that are taken for granted is not an easy task to get started. There is no motivation for someone who values high-performance sport to notice and then question how sport discipline forms athletic identities. It is unlikely that questioning will be taken seriously, even with the pedagogical prompting of a sport ethicist, unless participants experience and then notice some dissonance from the demands of other disciplines to which they are committed. Questions emerge once it is noticed that it is physically impossible to be engaged with the technologies of docility of one discipline – the particular organization of time, space, and modality of movement – while simultaneously engaged with the technologies of a competing discipline. If an athlete is to comply with the technologies of sport discipline, he or she cannot at the same time meet the time, space, and movement requirements of playing the piano or studying or, for female athletes, meet the conventional standards for her gender. When required to meet the demands of two or more disciplines simultaneously, one or more sets of demands 'necessarily fail.' It is impossible to satisfy 'a variety of different demands all at once.'[12] 'Necessary failures' occur because of the physical impossibility of being in more than one place and doing more than one activity at a time. Failure to meet the demands of a discipline also occurs because the values and desires embodied from other disciplines to which one is committed cannot just be thrown off. A discipline can never completely close the gaps required to achieve a completely disciplined performance because embodied skills and values from other disciplines, such as gender, sexuality, race, or class continually open gaps.

A responsibility of a new sport ethics is to make it possible for those implicated in sport discipline to notice that, despite their commitment, their participation is often disrupted by their hybrid interests. It is only by noticing these disruptions that participants can begin to question how they are implicated in the normalizing technologies of each of the disciplines to which they are subjected, give their assent to those features with which they agree, and refuse to conform to those processes of discipline with which they disagree. Since noticing disruptions also makes explicit the requirements of other disciplines to which participants are committed, a new sport ethics can open up questions about these disciplines as well, particularly how construction of identity through disciplines of gender, sexuality, class, race, and ability confound or conform to the demands of high-performance sport. This may lead to an exploration of how sport has contributed to the production of identity categories through sexist, homophobic, racist, and ableist practices.

Developing skills so that participants can read and interpret both representations from popular culture and texts from experts in sport is part of the larger project of a new sport ethics. Included in these skills are abilities to assess how values, interests, and identity are represented and produced through photographs, television, and video, and abilities to analyse texts as a means to identify what constitutes legitimate statements within a discourse, who benefits from the discourse, who has the right to speak, and what actions and interactions thereby are made possible. Becoming a skilled 'reader' of popular culture and texts of experts contributes to understanding, first, *that* knowledge, identities, and values are produced by the technologies and discourses of discipline and, then, '*how* knowledge is produced, identities shaped, and values articulated.'[13] This will require moving out of the strict disciplinary boundaries that have contained sport ethics and into multi- and interdisciplinary ways of noticing and questioning. Sport ethics will not be able to take on this work if it continues to rely solely on the skills of analytic philosophy.

Creating Alternative Athletic Identities: Playing with Identity

Questioning and refusal are central to ethics for Foucault, but he was also interested in creating something new. This 'something new' is 'not something that the individual invents by himself. They are patterns that he finds in his culture,'[14] but these 'patterns' can be extended to their limit, played with, reconfigured, and redeployed.[15] According to Foucault biographer James Miller, Foucault attempted to create something new in his own living by seeking out potentially transformative 'limit-experiences ... deliberately pushing his mind and body to the breaking point ... thus starkly revealing how distinctions central to the play of true and false are pliable, uncertain, contingent.'[16]

Pushing the limits of identity, thus creating new ways of understanding and participating in high-performance sport, will almost certainly be less ambitious than Foucault's limit-experiences. Sport ethics can, however, help participants, who are otherwise committed to skilled performance, identify when it might be possible to test the limits of their identities, both inside and outside competition. I have found it useful to explore with students how Dennis Rodman, bad boy of the National Basketball Association, represents himself as someone who pushes the limits of identity. Rodman claims that he wants 'to challenge people's image of what an athlete is supposed to be.'[17] On the court, Rodman displays multiple tattoos, dyed hair, and manicured and polished nails while paying much more attention to rebounding and defence than to scoring. In a sport whose heroes are measured by the number of points scored, Rodman says that he never wants to score.[18] He claims that he wants 'to be the first player in the game's history to average eighteen rebounds a game and only two points,' because it would be 'like turning the game on its head.'[19]

Off the court, Rodman cross-dresses or wears flamboyant clothes. He talks openly about going to gay bars and his fantasies about sex with men. Shortly after the release of his book, *Bad as I Wanna Be*, in the spring of 1996, Rodman appeared for a book signing in Chicago dressed in a silver halter, neon pink boa, and large silver earrings and wearing pink lipstick, pink fingernail polish, and silver hair. The caption under a newspaper photograph reads, 'Take It to the Limit.'[20] Later that summer for a book signing in New York, Rodman arrived in a horse-drawn carriage escorted by four women in tuxedos. He was wearing a blond wig, a white wedding gown, a nose piercing, and bright red lipstick. Rodman represents himself as 'looking for new ways to test myself ... There are no rules, no boundaries ... [M]ost people are afraid to let themselves go. They're afraid to take the chance, because they might find out something about themselves they don't really want to know.'[21]

What to make of this behaviour, outrageous in most contexts but particularly in the context of men's professional sport, which, in Rodman's own estimation, is 'a man's world'?[22] Is Dennis Rodman's cross-dressing an exploration of self, a protest over the NBA's rigid rules about marketing, a publicity stunt,[23] proof of a warped mind, or some of each of these? Most students thought Rodman to be 'crazy' or a 'troublemaker.' Many were unsympathetic to the suggestion that Rodman is attempting to push the limits of identity categories related to sport, sexuality, and gender. Rather, Rodman's antics had the effect with these students of solidifying notions of what is considered to be 'queer' and 'normal/abnormal' in this culture. Many students questioned Rodman's motivation and thought that he was attempting to draw attention to himself so he could better sell himself. They seemed unaware that, even while this may be his central motivation, performing 'queer' in a queer-unfriendly culture might have financial and safety risks. Rodman himself believes that he is underpaid by his employers and not considered for promotional contracts because he is not seen as a 'straight' player.

Whether his intention is to create new configurations of identity categories or to make more money or both, the effect of Dennis Rodman's performance of masculinity is disruptive of 'the male athlete.' Those who follow men's professional basketball cannot help but notice that his outstanding physical skills remain intact even though Rodman engages in some aspects of conventional femininity. This simultaneous performance of femininity and masculinity has the potential to create dissonance in some observers of Rodman. If this dissonance is noticed or recognized, there is the opportunity to begin questioning those practices that create and separate gendered identity. When it is acknowledged that Rodman wears dresses, has dated Madonna, and fantasizes about sex with men, and that he is the best rebounder in the NBA, it is possible for questions to emerge about the requirements of gendered performance and the relationship of gender to sexuality. Those who believe in a natural coherence of male sexed bodies with masculine gender performance and heterosexual sexual desire and practice will have this belief disrupted when faced with Rodman with his sizeable male body, 'masculine' basketball skills, 'feminine' dress, homosexual desire, and heterosexual practice.

Rodman's 'queerness' has the potential to disrupt dominant notions of the hyper-masculine black male and create new ways of understanding the category of race, but if this occurs, it is not because Rodman actively explores the limits of racial categories. Rodman plays with gender and sexuality, but he does little to confound notions of race. He says that he doesn't think about colour; that he tries to go beyond it, while acknowledging that 'some people won't let you go beyond it.'[24] He admits to playing 'the race card' when, after his rookie year in the NBA, he told the press that Larry Bird got the publicity he did because he is white. Rodman reports wishing to be white and not relating to black culture. He dates white women and comments that it is more common for a black man with status to date white women.[25] Rodman says that he believes that there is a double standard for black men with and without status, but he seems unaware that 'white' still confers status in this culture, which is why he gains status when he dates white women. It seems not to have occurred to Rodman to push the limits of 'race' in order to turn standards of white and black on their head. Or perhaps, if the students in my courses are correct, he's not interested in this because there is no money in pushing the limits of race.

Noticing, questioning, and affirming or refusing how discipline constructs identity are difficult tasks, but they can be systematically addressed by a new sport ethics. It is less obvious how sport ethics can assist participants in creating new ways of participating in high-performance sport. Few are in the position to be as flamboyant as Dennis Rodman and not be dismissed from teams. It may be possible, however, for sport participants to experiment with some features of identity and in doing so create variations of that identity. To get at what I mean by this, it is important to recall that in earlier chapters I described how identity, including athletic, gendered, sexual, and racial identity, is stabilized by repetitive performance of comportment, movements, gestures, and expressions. Here, I am suggesting that it is possible to destabilize or disrupt identity by altering these repetitions – that is, by playing with or parodying performances of gender, sexuality, race, and/or athletic ability.[26]

Expectations for conventional femininity and expectations for athletes are already disrupted by female athletes participating in high-performance sport, as are expectations for conventional masculinity when gay men participate in high-performance sport. These disruptions can be magnified when expected performances are played with or parodied. For example, members of the Beehives, a women's hockey team with 'big hair'[27] parody both femininity and 'masculine' sport by representing themselves as hyper-feminine in appearance while performing a sport that requires skills of conventional masculinity. As one player reports, 'the big hair thing flies in the face of how hockey players usually define themselves – macho, virile, all of that. Beehives are a contradiction in terms: we are ... women with a femmy icon who can REALLY play hockey.'[28]

There is no guarantee, however, that these disruptions will create new ways of understanding or participating in sport for others because, as Judith Butler writes, 'practices of parody can serve to reengage and reconsolidate the very distinction'[29] between what is thought to be 'natural' and what is thought to be contrived. In the case of the Beehives, as in the case of Dennis Rodman, some 'readers' of these performances will take the dissonance between expected performance and actual performance as a prompt to question why and how these expectations have been structured in the way they have. Others will experience dissonance as proof of the 'queerness' of those who cannot get 'natural' gender or conventional sport performance right.

I started thinking about the implications of playing with athletic identities after a skit about the Gay Games was performed at a student retreat. Those in the skit performed an exaggerated stereotype of a gay man – 'feminine,' unfamiliar and uncomfortable with attempting 'masculine' sport activities. The skit was amusing to many at the retreat because the parody occurred in a context in which confusions about gender could be fostered.[30] The confusions did not subvert gender, sexuality, or athletic identity, however, because the actors in the skit assumed themselves to be 'real' or 'normal' men engaged in a parody of 'abnormal' men attempting sport skills.[31] That many at the retreat found the parody amusing demonstrates that playing with identity does not necessarily create new ways of understanding or participating in sport. Indeed, in this case, because masculine and athletic identities were assumed to be 'real' or 'natural,' playing with identity by the actors in the skit confirmed the perversity or deviance of those who do not get identity 'right.'

A picture from my local newspaper shows a man in drag competing in the 'wild drag race' event at the Gay Rodeo. He is dragging what appears to be a full-grown steer while wearing a chiffon dress, gloves, a crown, and sneakers. It is not clear from the photograph whether this is a 'feminine' man participating in sport, a parody of a 'feminine' man in sport, a 'casual and cynical mockery of women,'[32] or a spoof on 'masculine' men. Since the subversiveness of parody 'depends upon a context and reception in which subversive confusions can be fostered,'[33] it is possible for the man in drag participating in the gay rodeo to be 'read' as a spoof on rodeo, as an insult to women, as a spoof on the artifice of gender, or as a consolidation of gayness as perverse and of a notion of what rodeo 'really' looks like when 'real' men participate.[34] Only some of these readings have the potential to create new ways of understanding or participating in high-performance sport.

When masculine men or athletic women parody feminine women performing sport skills, it is unlikely that this parody will create new ways of understanding or performing established identity categories. When a

feminine woman is represented as throwing, running, climbing, swinging, or hitting 'like a girl' by masculine men or athletic women, this parody consolidates the notion of the physically limited feminine woman.
Moreover, when athletic women have some investment in their own femininity, at least outside athletic performance, a parody of feminine women
performing sport skills is more like a joke on themselves because it draws
attention to inconsistencies in their femininity. This is particularly the
case if a dark-skinned female athlete parodies a white feminine woman
attempting sport skills. While the parody might expose the artifice of femininity and the racist assumptions configured in femininity, the parody
also runs the risk of reconfiguring the dark-skinned woman as 'deficient'
as a woman – that is, as masculine.

Parody of conventional masculinity by a male who takes his masculinity
seriously is also ineffective in creating new ways of understanding or
participating in sport because, in imitating himself, a masculine male is
indistinguishable from himself.[35] When someone's identity matches the
expectations for that identity, it is difficult to recognize the repetitive performances that go into solidifying identity as performance. The performance does not look like a performance because it 'effects realness, to
the extent that it *cannot* be read ... where what appears and what it means
coincide.'[36] Men in drag and feminine women *are* in a position to subvert
the perceived naturalness of masculine men and create new ways of
understanding and participating in sport because the 'artifice of the performance can be read as artifice.'[37] Since in most contexts neither men in
drag nor feminine women are perceived to be able to perform sport
skills, when they exaggerate the masculinity of men in sport, it is possible
to disrupt the assumption that masculinity 'naturally' coheres to male
bodies.

It has occurred to me to wonder what might have happened if the
theme 'Gay Games' had been given to athletic women with the expectation that they parody lesbians in sport and to wonder whether their parody would create any new possibilities for sport. Like masculine men
attempting to parody masculine men, an athletic woman looks 'real' as
she attempts her parody of the lesbian or dyke in sport. An athletic
woman looks like an athletic woman as she attempts a parody of 'the dyke
in sport' because characteristics of a lesbian in sport – aggressive, strong,
skilled – are also characteristics of an athletic woman.[38]

While a gay man in drag can use sport as a context to parody gender and sport and create new possibilities for understanding and participating in sport, it is much more difficult for a lesbian to use sport as a context to create something new. Since 'drag' on a female body is thought to consist of 'masculine' attire and bodily comportment, a lesbian in drag is indistinguishable from a lesbian in sport and, from the more general category, the athletic woman in sport. A lesbian athlete may, however, consider herself to be in drag when wearing 'feminine' apparel. She might wear a pink tutu while running and winning the 200-metre sprint event, something that occurred at the 1994 New York Gay Games. By doing so, she may not only subvert stereotypes of lesbians in sport but also introduce another level of questions about the relationship of femininity to masculinity in sport and, perhaps like the Beehives, open up new ways to participate in sport.

Pushing the limits of identity has been open to athletes, like Dennis Rodman, whose worth as a professional athlete makes it possible for him to engage in practices disruptive to established identity categories without losing his spot on the team. The Beehives, the cowboy in the Gay Rodeo, and the sprinter at the Gay Games are able to parody gendered, sexual, and athletic identity while they are competing because pushing the limits of identity is in part what the team or the competition is fostering. Most athletes, however, must not only comply with the sport skill requirements of 'the athlete,' they must also comply with the expectations associated with their gender and race or not be regarded as 'good' team-mates. Moreover, for athletes with disabilities, the limitations imposed by impairment make it impossible to parody able-bodied athletes in or out of competition.[39]

Despite the few opportunities to play with identity, new ways of participating in high-performance sport nevertheless are created. Diverse, hybrid participants configure new identities for high-performance sport by virtue of their involvement in other disciplines. Encouraging diversity may, then, be the most effective way a new sport ethics has to intervene in modern sport and create something new.

Proliferating Diversity

Possibilities for a new sport ethics emerge from the disruptions that occur when the hybrid interests of athletes come up against the demands of sport. By noticing these disruptions and both questioning and refusing passive compliance with discipline, participants are in a position to make decisions about how they will participate in high-performance sport. Hybrid athletes will contend in hybrid ways with the dissonance they feel as a result of failure to meet the conflicting demands of disciplines to which they are committed. Some female athletes, for example, may be willing to live with ambiguities that arise when the demands of sport discipline and conventional femininity cannot be met, or they may refuse certain technologies of sport or femininity that create these ambiguities. Athletes who experience less ambiguity, as may be the case for some male athletes, may see no point in refusing identity. Still others may value their athletic identities but wish to question and actively alter the ways in which technologies of identity are controlled by experts. Questioning may lead others to a refusal of the ways in which identity is constructed, represented, and imposed by sport discipline.[40] When a participant questions the normalizing processes of sport discipline and refuses those with which he or she cannot comply, a new configuration of sport participation is created for that participant.

Without hybridity and diversity, disruptions and hence questioning and refusal are less likely to occur. Diversity and hybridity are antidotes for the potential totalizing effects of discipline. If sport ethics is to accomplish the pedagogical task of making it possible for participants to notice disruptions, to question and refuse discipline, and perhaps create something new, it is my contention that sport ethics must also assume the political task of promoting a diverse population of participants with hybrid interests.[41] This is particularly important in sport for children and youth, where requirements that children have few interests outside of sport reduce demands from other disciplines and where requirements for a narrow range of acceptable body types, including implicit acceptance of light skin as an aesthetic standard, especially in 'aesthetic' sports for girls, reduce the potential diversity of participants.

I am aware that some will see disruption of the demands of high-performance sport as an argument for reducing rather than increasing the diversity of athletes and for recruiting and supporting athletes with few interests outside sport. Like political struggles over diversity in workplaces, legislatures, courts of law, and communities, diversity will not be welcomed by those who want participants to be homogeneous since 'common' goals are more readily achievable when values, interests, and desires are the same. If sport ethics is not to continue to be a 'powerless protest against sport,'[42] an important task of sport ethics will be to upset this homogeneity.

This brings me to the end of the tasks I set out for myself. I wanted to make sense of the production of highly expert skill and knowledge in sport discipline by taking up Michel Foucault's work on disciplinary power. Foucault's map of disciplinary technology has been helpful in understanding the extent to which technologies of discipline permeate athletes' bodies, producing exquisite skill. I also wanted to acknowledge what was apparent to me as someone implicated for so many years in high-performance sport – that despite the relentlessness of the technologies of sport discipline, the hybridity and diversity of participants guarantee that no one participates in high-performance sport in the same way and that no one is ever consumed by sport discipline. This dissonance between what modern sport attempts to accomplish and what it can accomplish in a postmodern context of diversity creates the space for postmodern interventions. Taking the lead from Foucault, this is an ethics that questions the demands of high-performance sport, refuses those demands that contradict other important values, and thereby creates the possibility of new ways of understanding and participating in high-performance sport.

Notes

Preface

1 See Andrews, 'Desperately Seeking Michel'; Cole, 'Resisting the Canon';
   Heikkala, 'Discipline and Excel'; Rail and Harvey, 'Body at Work'; and
   Vigarello, 'The Life of the Body.'
2 See Frye, *The Politics of Reality*; Sherwin, *No Longer Patient*; Shogan, 'Conceptualizing Agency'; and Tong, *Feminine and Feminist Ethics.*

Chapter One: Introduction

1 Fraser, *Unruly Practices*, 20
2 Foucault, *Discipline and Punish*, 194
3 Fraser, *Unruly Practices*, 20, emphasis added
4 In a non-game context such as schooling, constraints produce what is to count
   as teaching and learning; skills that are appropriate for each level of teaching
   and learning; and appropriate behaviours between and among students and
   between students and teachers. These prescriptive constraints produce actions
   that in part constitute the identities of 'student' and 'teacher.' A number of
   other constraints further circumscribe these identities by proscribing or prohibiting certain actions – for example, students must not be late, miss class, be
   disruptive, talk out of turn, or be disrespectful to the teacher. These actions
   often take place in the context of a school with partitioned rooms containing
   desks for each student and teacher. Rooms may have blackboards, computers,
   libraries, labs, and equipment. The extent to which these are present or
   absent circumscribes teaching and learning and which skills will be produced.
   Schooling also takes place in the suburbs or the inner city and in the context
   of attitudes toward racial, gender, class, and sexuality politics. Each of these

'descriptive contexts' differentially constrains the actions of individuals in schools.

5 As I elaborate in the next chapter, by technological intervention I simply mean an organized, systematic, expert application of techniques, mechanisms, or practices designed to normalize or standardize performance or behaviour.

6 Usher and Edwards, *Postmodernism and Education*, 82

7 Lyon, *Postmodernity*, 18. As indicated by Dean, *Critical and Effective Histories*, 7, modernity has also been associated with one or more of the following: 'industrial technology, ... bureaucratic modes of administration, urbanism, the liberal-democratic state, affective individualism, the public/private dichotomy, and so on. These accounts then give rise to the host of process terms which circumscribe different features of this great transformation: modernisation, industrialisation, rationalisation, urbanisation, secularisation, bureaucratisation, etc.'

8 Foucault, *History of Sexuality, Volume I*, 139

9 Foucault, *Discipline and Punish*, 136

10 Foucault, 'Two Lectures,' 104

11 Foucault, *Discipline and Punish*, 137, 138

12 Foucault, 'The Subject and Power,' 217, emphasis in original

13 Bale, *Landscapes of Modern Sport*, 2. Included in highly rationalized sport was a change in the physical environment that was to be used exclusively by sport. As Bale writes on p. 39, 'during the eighteenth and nineteenth centuries the landscape of sport became increasingly artificial as science and technology "improved" the cultivation of sports, just as they were improving the cultivation of wheat, barley, sheep, and cattle.'

14 Foucault, *Discipline and Punish*, 141

15 Foucault, 'Two Lectures,' 106

16 The congruence between Foucault's description of the technologies of discipline and sport discipline prompted a graduate student in Sport Studies to remark that he thought that Foucault must have been a coach.

17 Ravizza and Daruty, 'Paternalism and Sovereignty in Athletics'; Thomas, 'Criteria for Athlete Autonomy in a Paternalistic Sport Model'

18 Foucault, *History of Sexuality, Volume I*, 82; *Discipline and Punish*, 138

19 Marshall, 'Foucault and Education,' 107

20 Foucault, *Discipline and Punish*, 27

21 Foucault, 'Two Lectures,' 93

22 Dreyfus and Rabinow, *Michel Foucault*, 66

23 Foucault, *The Archaeology of Knowledge*, 116

24 Shumway, *Michel Foucault*, 10

25 Foucault, *The Archaelogy of Knowlege*, 51

26 Foucault, 'Truth and Power,' 131
27 Flax, 'The End of Innocence,' 452
28 Shogan, 'Comments on Hawkesworth's "Knowers, Knowing, Known,"' 424
29 Heikkala, 'Discipline and Excel,' 401
30 Vigarello, 'The Life of the Body in *Discipline and Punish*,' 158
31 Fiske, 'Bodies of Knowledge,' 64
32 Ibid., 163
33 See Polanyi, *Personal Knowledge*; Kleinman, 'The Significance of Human Movement'; and Hirst, *Knowledge and the Curriculum.*
34 Baier, 'Trust and Antitrust'

Chapter Two: Production of 'The Athlete'

1 Foucault, *Discipline and Punish*, 141
2 Fiske, 'Bodies of Knowledge,' 74
3 Foucault, *Discipline and Punish*, 137
4 Ibid., 140
5 Bale, *Landscapes of Modern Sport*, 67
6 Ibid., 2
7 Foucault, *Discipline and Punish*, 147
8 Ibid.
9 Shogan, 'Alberta's Combination Press,' 64
10 Foucault, *Discipline and Punish*, 142
11 Ibid., 143
12 Ibid.
13 Ibid.
14 Ibid., 144
15 Shogan, 'Alberta's Combination Press,' 64
16 Foucault, *Discipline and Punish*, 147
17 Ibid., 148
18 Ibid.
19 In *Landscapes of Modern Sport*, 75, Bale writes that enclosures that separated playing space from space occupied by spectators 'provided the final break with the pre-modern traditions and can therefore be seen as marking (literally) the emergence of sporting modernity.'
20 Townley, *Reframing Human Resource Management*, 52
21 Tronchot quoted in Foucault, *Discipline and Punish*, 150
22 Warren and Chapman, *Basketball Coach's Survival Guide*, 124–5
23 Foucault, *Discipline and Punish*, 151
24 Ibid., 150, 151

25 Coaching Association of Canada, *NCCP Theory II*, 6, 2; emphasis in original
26 Foucault, *Discipline and Punish*, 150
27 *Ordonnance* quoted in Foucault, *Discipline and Punish*, 151
28 Foucault, *Discipline and Punish*, 152
29 Ibid.
30 Ibid., 151
31 Ibid., 152
32 Shogan, Instructional Video
33 Foucault, *Discipline and Punish*, 152
34 Ibid.
35 *Ordonnance* quoted in Foucault, *Discipline and Punish*, 153
36 Foucault, *Discipline and Punish*, 153
37 Shogan, instructional video
38 Foucault, *Discipline and Punish*, 153
39 Ibid., 154
40 Ibid.
41 Ibid.
42 Ibid.
43 Ibid., 157
44 Townley, *Reframing Human Resource Management*, 74
45 Foucault, *Discipline and Punish*, 157
46 Townley, *Reframing Human Resource Management*, 74
47 Foucault, *Discipline and Punish*, 162
48 Ibid., 157
49 Ibid., 158
50 Ibid.
51 Warren and Chapman, *Basketball Coach's Survival Guide*, 139–44
52 Townley, *Reframing Human Resource Management*, 74
53 Foucault, *Discipline and Punish*, 158
54 Ibid.
55 Ibid.
56 Ibid., 158–9
57 Ibid., 164
58 Ibid., 163
59 Ibid., 164
60 Ibid.
61 Ibid.
62 Ibid., 165
63 Ibid., 166
64 Ibid.

65 Ibid.
66 Ibid.
67 Ibid., 170
68 Ibid., 172
69 L.J. Davis, *Enforcing Normalcy*, 30
70 Heikkala, 'Discipline and Excel,' 400
71 Foucault, *Discipline and Punish*, 182
72 Heikkala, 'Discipline and Excel,' 400
73 Foucault, *Discipline and Punish*, 202–3
74 Ibid., 205
75 Ibid., 200
76 Ibid., 205
77 Fiske, 'Bodies of Knowledge,' 72
78 Canadian Centre for Drug-Free Sport, *Guide to Drug Free Sport*, 6
79 Fox, Bowers, and Foss, *The Physiological Basis for Exercise and Sport*, v–xiii
80 Kreighbaum and Barthels, *Biomechanics*, viii–ix
81 Magill, *Motor Learning*, viii
82 Fiske, 'Bodies of Knowledge,' 72
83 Often students and professors of sport studies are concerned with what they believe to be an inaccurate representation of their academic program. In order to be regarded as experts of sport science and not (merely) as performers of sport, students and professors do a kind of confessing that these programs focus on acquisition of a range of propositional knowledges in biomechanics, the physiology of exercise, training and conditioning, and motor performance – and not on physical activity. While such a stance is perhaps astute in a university culture that values propositional knowledges over procedural knowledges, it strikes me as curious that those interested in the enhancement of sport performance should argue that what legitimates the discipline of sport studies is knowledge about performance enhancement rather than performance itself. In my opinion, devaluing the procedural knowledge of performance and placing a superior value on propositional knowledges about performance enhancement contributes to the asssumption that athletes are more controlled by sport discipline than are sport scientists and coaches.
84 Legitimate talk in high-performance sport focuses on the science of performance, which produces 'an ethos of professional expertise, a reliance on scientistic teaching methodologies, and an obsession with instrumental rationality ... [that] results in the framing of highly selective definitions of health, fitness, the body, sport and physical education by intellectual gatekeepers.' See McKay, Gore, and Kirk, 'Beyond the Limits of Technocratic Physical

Education,' 53. Concerns of McKay, Gore, and Kirk's with physical education are magnified in sport discipline, in which the science of performance is explicit.

85 Coaching Association of Canada, *NCCP I*, 6–6
86 Townley, *Reframing Human Resource Management*, 111
87 Foucault, *The History of Sexuality, Volume I*, 61–2
88 Nideffer, 'Attentional Focus – Self Assessment,' 281
89 Usher and Edwards, *Postmodernism and Education*, 10
90 Bauman, *Intimations of Postmodernity*, 35
91 Real, 'The Postmodern Olympics,' 19
92 Ibid., 9
93 Ibid., 22

Chapter Three: Hybrid Athletes

1 Frye, *The Politics of Reality*, 22
2 Grimshaw, *Philosophy and Feminist Thinking*
3 Ibid., 62
4 Scott, 'Experience,' 25
5 Ibid.
6 Foucault, 'Two Lectures,' 107; emphasis in orginal
7 Foucault, *Discipline and Punish*, 182
8 L.J. Davis, *Enforcing Normalcy*; Hacking, 'Was There a Probabilistic Revolution?' and *The Taming of Chance*; MacKenzie, *Statistics in Britain*. I am indebted to Sheryl McInnes for drawing my attention to literature in the history of statistics.
9 Davis, *Enforcing Normalcy*, 24
10 Davis, *Enforcing Normalcy*; Hacking, 'Was There a Probabilistic Revolution?'
11 Davis, *Enforcing Normalcy*; Hacking, *The Taming of Chance*
12 Ibid.
13 Davis, *Enforcing Normalcy*
14 Ibid., 30, 29
15 Cited in Porter, *The Rise of Statistical Thinking*, 103
16 Davis, *Enforcing Normalcy*, 34
17 Ibid., 24
18 Hacking, *The Taming of Chance*
19 Ibid.
20 Davis, *Enforcing Normalcy*; MacKenzie, *Statistics in Britain*
21 Davis, *Enforcing Normalcy*, 30
22 McDermott and Varenne, 'Culture *as* Disability,' 337

23 Dreyfus and Rabinow, *Michel Foucault*, 258
24 Davis, *Enforcing Normalcy*, 30
25 Landers, 'Column,' C6
26 Young, 'Throwing Like a Girl,' 137
27 Ibid., 142
28 Whitson, 'Sport in the Social Construction of Masculinity,' 23
29 Sabo, 'The Politics of Homophobia in Sport,' 86
30 Messner, *Power at Play*, 64
31 Connell, *Which Way Is Up?* 19
32 Young, 'Throwing Like a Girl,' 142
33 Ibid., 143
34 Messner, 'Ah, Ya Throw Like A Girl!' 30
35 Young, 'Throwing Like a Girl,' 152
36 Ibid., 153
37 Sedgwick, *Tendencies*, 158
38 Burke, *Gender Shock*, 5
39 Ibid.
40 Ibid., 19. These interventions are recommended to doctors in Ruckers's *Handbook of Child and Adolescent Sexual Problems*, published in 1995.
41 Burke, *Gender Shock*, 19
42 Bartky, 'Foucault, Femininity,' 65
43 Ibid., 71
44 Ibid.
45 Feminine 'men' are also highly skilled in the discipline of femininity. Drag queens and transsexuals require these skills in order to perform their femininity.
46 Bartky, 'Foucault, Femininity,' 77
47 Duncan, 'The Politics of Women's Body Images,' 51
48 Ibid., 49
49 Morgan, 'Women and the Knife,' 31
50 Bordo, 'Reading the Slender Body,' 85
51 Connell, *Which Way Is Up?* 20
52 Whitson, 'Sport in the Social Construction of Masculinity,' 19
53 Connell, *Which Way Is Up?*
54 Whitson, 'Sport in the Social Construction of Masculinity,' 22
55 Bartky, 'Foucault, Femininity,' 80
56 Ibid., 65
57 Ibid.
58 Ibid.
59 Deveaux, 'Feminism and Empowerment,' 227

60 Bleier, *Science and Gender*, vii. Some scientists and social scientists still are in the business of devising ways to measure, demonstrate, and establish two discrete sexes in order to establish biological bases for differences in social, economic, and political positions. There are also research programs to establish biological bases to explain and politically differentiate sexuality and race.

61 Butler, 'Sex and Gender in Simone de Beauvoir's *Second Sex*,' 35

62 Butler, *Gender Trouble*, 17

63 Ibid., 8

64 Butler, *Gender Trouble*

65 Ibid.

66 Bartky, 'Foucault, Femininity,' 68

67 Butler, *Gender Trouble*, 32

68 Warner, *Fear of a Queer Planet*, xxi

69 See Brian Pronger's discussion of 'receptive men' in *The Arena of Masculinity*, 136–41.

70 Whitson, 'Sport in the Social Construction of Masculinity,' 23

71 Burke, *Gender Shock*, 5

72 Ibid., 205

73 See Kidd, 'Sports and Masculinity'; Messner, *Power at Play*; Messner and Sabo, *Sex, Violence & Power in Sports*; Pronger, 'Gay Jocks'; and Whitson, 'Sport in the Social Construction of Masculinity,' and 'The Embodiment of Gender.'

74 Whitson, 'Sport in the Social Construction of Masculinity,' 19

75 Whitson, 'The Embodiment of Gender,' 359

76 Burke, *Gender Shock*, 204

77 Leibovitz, 'An Olympic Portfolio,' 152

78 See, for example, Cahn, *Coming On Strong*; Creedon, *Women, Media and Sport*; Hargreaves, *Sporting Females*; and Lenskyj, *Out of Bounds*.

79 Cahn, *Coming On Strong*

80 Hargreaves, *Sporting Females*, 222

81 Daniels, 'Gender (Body) Verification (Building),' 375

82 Hargreaves, *Sporting Females*, 222

83 Daniels, 'Gender (Body) Verification (Building),' 374

84 Hood-Williams, 'Sexing the Athletes,' 301

85 Fausto-Sterling, *Myths of Gender*

86 Davis and Delano, 'Fixing the Boundaries of Physical Gender,' 90

87 Ibid., 11

88 Pronger, 'Gay Jocks,' 149

89 Sabo, 'The Politics of Homophobia in Sport,' 103–4

90 Cam Cole, 'Men Making Moves in a New Arena,' A1

91 Adams, 'Real Men Don't Wear Sequins'

 92 Cole, 'Men Making Moves in a New Arena,' A12
 93 Cahn, *Coming On Strong*, 268
 94 Brownworth, 'The Competitive Closet,' 79
 95 Ibid.
 96 Messner, 'Gay Athletes and the Gay Games,' 116
 97 Cahn, *Coming On Strong*, 206
 98 Ibid., 190
 99 Berger, 'The Suit and the Photograph'
100 Ibid., 428
101 Ibid., 431
102 Frye, 'White Woman Feminist'
103 Ibid., 151–2; emphasis in original
104 Quoted in Begley, 'Three Is Not Enough,' 67.
105 Haug, *Female Sexualization*, 173
106 For purposes of illustration, I focus on 'blackliness' and blackness, while acknowledging that other 'races' also materialize from expected performances.
107 Fanon, *Black Skin White Masks*, 166. It is important to emphasize that the culturally dominant materialization of 'blackness' is what appears in the 'white imagination.' See hooks, 'Representing Whiteness in the Black Imagination' for an 'ethnographic account' of the ways in which black people conceptualize whiteness.
108 See Marilyn Frye's discussion of white people as judgers, preachers, and peacekeepers in 'White Woman Feminist,' 153–7.
109 Majors, 'Cool Pose'
110 Ibid., 111
111 hooks, *Outlaw Culture*, 180
112 Cahn, *Coming On Strong*, 127
113 Ibid., 127–8
114 As quoted by Nickson, 'She's Not Heavy, She's My Sister,' D3
115 Reported by Nickson, ibid.
116 Williams, *The Rooster's Egg*, 37–8
117 Andrews, 'The Facts of Michael Jordan's Blackness,' 138
118 Ibid., 137
119 Hernstein and Murray, *The Bell Curve*
120 Rees, 'Race and Sport in Global Perspective,' 22
121 Cahn, *Coming On Strong*, 128
122 Majors, 'Cool Pose,' 110
123 Birrell, 'Racial Relations Theories and Sport,' 213
124 Hall, 'White Identities,' 114

125 Hoberman, *Darwin's Athletes*, 223
126 Ibid., 224
127 This was the question posed on the cover of *Newsweek*, 13 Feb. 1995.
128 United Nations, *World Programme of Action*, I.c. 6–7; emphasis added
129 Wendell, 'Toward a Feminist Theory of Disability,' 107
130 Oliver, *Understanding Disability*, 22
131 Wendell, 'Toward a Feminist Theory of Disability,' 107
132 Ibid., 109, 107
133 Davis, *Enforcing Normalcy*, 3
134 McDermott and Varenne, 'Culture *as* Disability,' 337
135 Ibid., 327–8
136 Groce, reported in McDermott and Varenne, 'Culture *as* Disability,' 328
137 Ibid.
138 Wendell, 'Toward a Feminist Theory of Disability,' 108
139 Dunn, *Special Physical Education*
140 Cronon, *Uncommon Ground*, 36
141 Vanlandewijck and Chappel, 'Integration and Classification Issues,' 70
142 Davis, *Enforcing Normalcy*, 269
143 Men who are unathletic, however, are not presumed to be genetic females. Regardless of how poorly skilled or unathletic an individual man is, he is identified with the characteristics of the most skilled and athletic men. See Shogan, 'Inequality in Sport,' 273.
144 DePauw and Gavron, *Disability and Sport*, 204
145 Lindstrom, 'Sports Classification for Locomotor Disabilities,' 134. My example added.
146 Ibid.
147 Ibid., 132
148 Chang, 'A Not-So-New Spelling of My Name,' 260
149 Haraway, ' A Cyborg Manifesto,' 178
150 As Donna Haraway indicates, cyborgs are not innocent or good. Technologies that create cyborgs can solidify binaries as well. When cosmetic surgery, for example, is used to conform to notions of conventional femininty, the cyborg created contributes to the female/male binary.
151 Butler, *Gender Trouble*, 145

Chapter Four: Ethical Issues and the Scholarly Field of Sport Ethics

1 Attempts to develop children's ethical skills involve the organization of time, space, and movement so that they attend to what is valued in their culture and can practise actions or skills that are assessed against an ethical standard.

2 Murdoch, *The Sovereignty of Good*, 67
3 While traditional philosophy makes claims for the universality of ethical
   standards for ethics, many of the standards against which ethical 'goodness'
   or 'rightness' are measured are culturally different for females and males,
   with the 'universal' standard coinciding with the standards attributed to
   men. Carol Gilligan found, for example, that the girls and women she
   studied tended to adjudicate conflicts by emphasizing relationships and
   connection, while boys and men tended to adjudicate conflicts by emphasizing rights and autonomy. For girls and women, regular attention to
   what 'good' women do and messages about the importance of caring, nurturing, and self-sacrifice for the good of others set both the standard against
   which girls and women measure themselves and contribute to the
   embodiment of desires to meet this standard. See Gilligan, *In a Different
   Voice.*

   Nurturing as a feminine value may be more predominant in middle-class
   women than in working-class women. See Martindale, 'Theorizing Autobiography.' Sandra Harding cites studies which show that many African men
   respond to ethical situations in a way similar to many women in North American studies, and she argues that these 'caring' responses reflect an orientation
   of those who exercise less power in relation to those who exercise more power.
   Harding contends that those who exercise less power are 'caring,' 'nice,' and
   'polite' toward those who exercise more power as a way to negotiate interactions with those who could thwart or harm them in some way. What would be
   telling is a study of white women's interactions with, say, men of colour in a
   context in which these women exercise more power. If Harding is correct, the
   men of colour will demonstrate 'caring' behaviours in relation to these white
   women and the white women will interact with these men of colour in terms of
   principles of fairness. See Harding, 'The Curious Coincidence of Feminine
   and African Moralities.'
4 See Foucault, *History of Sexuality, Volume I*, 184 and *Power/Knowledge*, 93, 95, and
   Fraser, *Unruly Practices*, 21.
5 König, 'Criticism of Doping,' 251
6 Ibid., 252
7 Pearson, 'Deception, Sportsmanship, and Ethics,' 265
8 Suits, *The Grasshopper: Games, Life and Utopia*, 24
9 König, 'Criticism of Doping,' 253
10 Shogan, 'The Prisoner's Dilemma in Competitive Sport'
11 Larson and LaFasto, *TeamWork*
12 Carron, 'Cohesion in Team Sports'
13 Syer, *Team Spirit*

14 Larson and LaFasto, *TeamWork*; Schellenberger, *Psychology of Team Sports*; Syer, *Team Spirit*

15 Syer, *Team Spirit*, 17

16 Larson and LaFasto, *TeamWork*, 84

17 J. Brown, quoted in Syer, *Team Spirit*, 98

18 Larson and LaFasto, *TeamWork*, 88

19 Ibid., 89, 88

20 Ibid., 88

21 Schellenberger, *Psychology of Team Sports*

22 Messner, *Power at Play*, 88

23 Cornell, *The Philosophy of the Limit*, 1

24 Ibid.; emphasis added

25 Butler, 'Contingent Foundations,' 15

26 Pronger, 'Gay Jocks,' 147

27 Baier, 'Trust and Antitrust'

28 Ibid., 234

29 Ibid., 252

30 When equals are in a relationship of trust, a betrayal of trust is often very hurtful to the person betrayed, yet individuals in the relationship are not bound to maintain the relationship even while betrayed. When a betrayal of trust occurs by someone who exercises more power, betrayal is hurtful to the person betrayed, the relationship is undermined, and the betrayed person often has no other choice but to stay in the relationship in some way. When a coach is not trustworthy, an athlete often must stay in the relationship or not compete.

31 Baier, 'Trust and Antitrust,' 235

32 Ibid., 236

33 Ibid., 237

34 Ibid., 238

35 Ibid., 231–2

36 Ibid., 255

37 Ibid., 259, emphasis in original

38 Ibid., 255

39 Ibid., 256

40 Ibid.

41 Ford, 'Distrusting Gender,' n.p.

42 Davies and Lonsbrough, 'Lost Chance to Halt the Rapist Coach,' 3

43 McCarten, 'Report of Sexual Abuse Shatters Hockey World,' D3

44 The work of Pat Galasso is an exception. See Galasso, 'Children in Organized Sport.'

45 König, 'Criticism of Doping,' 256
46 Ibid.

Chapter Five: Hybrid Athletes and Discipline

1 Foucault, 'Power and Strategies,' 142
2 See Filax, 'Critical Pedagogy and Resistance'
3 This organization, now called Athletes CAN, was previously the Canadian Athletes' Association (CAA).
4 See Weedon, *Feminist Practice and Poststructuralist Theory*, for a discussion about the ways in which creation of identity produces the discursive space from which someone can resist his or her subjectification.
5 Foucault, *The Use of Pleasure*, 29–30
6 Ibid., 26
7 Foucault, 'What Is Enlightenment?' 46
8 Foucault, 'The Subject and Power,' 216
9 Foucault, *The Use of Pleasure*, 26
10 Ibid., 27–8
11 Foucault, 'What Is Enlightenment?' 45
12 Butler, *Gender Trouble*, 145
13 Giroux, *Disturbing Pleasures*, 22; emphasis added
14 Foucault, 'The Ethic of Care for the Self,' 11
15 Butler, *Gender Trouble*, 145
16 Miller, *The Passion of Michel Foucault*, 30
17 Rodman, *Bad as I Wanna Be*, 166
18 Ibid., 107
19 Ibid., 111. Rodman has made it possible to consider defence and rebounding as legitimate measures of skilled performance in basketball. If limits of what counts as skill were pushed in synchronized swimming, acknowledgment of underwater strength and musculature could come to be included in the assessment of skilled performance.
20 Edmonton *Journal,* 'Taking It to the Limit,' D6
21 Ibid., 166–7
22 Rodman, *Bad as I Wanna Be*, 166
23 Christie, 'Basketball's Purist Bares All,' C3
24 Rodman, *Bad as I Wanna Be*, 135
25 Ibid., 143
26 Butler, *Gender Trouble*, 146–7
27 Roxxie, 'Hockey Action: Beehives!' 14
28 Ibid., 15

29 Butler, *Gender Trouble*, 146
30 Ibid., 139
31 The parody was successful because of several shared assumptions: assumptions about the coherence of sexed bodies, gender, and sexuality; assumptions that sport is a forum within which masculine or 'real' men are able to demonstrate abilities constitutive of masculinity – aggression, strength, skilfulness; assumptions that 'real' or feminine women lack these constitutive abilities; and assumptions that gay men are gay because they lack constitutive masculine abilities (a view of homosexuality as 'sexual inversion'). Another likely assumption of this parody was that participants in the Gay Games are 'white' gay men. Because of cultural myths about the 'hyper-masculinity' and 'hyper(hetero)sexuality' of black males and an appropriation and reconfiguration of these stereotypes by many black males, the possibility of a black effeminate male athlete is outside the imagination of most in this culture.
32 Frye, *The Politics of Reality*, 137. Butler writes that a feminist analysis that 'diagnoses male homosexuality as rooted in misogyny ... is a way for feminist women to make themselves into the center of male homosexual activity (and thus to reinscribe the heterosexual matrix ...).' See Butler, *Bodies That Matter*, 127
33 Butler, *Gender Trouble*, 139
34 It is possible that the drag queen participating in the gay rodeo might be 'read' as a parody of women in sport, although such a parody is subversive only if it is apparent that women's sport is being spoofed – something like the representation of a women's baseball game that appeared on the cover of the *Harvard Lampoon* several years ago in which the female catcher had her baseball cap on backwards to accommodate her baseball mask and her breasts were turned backwards to accommodate her chest pad.
35 White masculine males and black masculine males might parody each other, making it possible that some might notice that masculinity is racialized. As Richard Majors argues in 'Cool Pose,' black 'cool pose' is a performance that white males are likely to fail to copy. Because the virtuoso performances cultivated by black male athletes are valued widely by sport enthusiasts, impersonations of black male athletes by white men, unlike other stereotypical impersonations of blacks by whites, may appear respectful – like any attempt at modelling skills that are admired. By contrast, impersonations of white male athletes by black males are open to a kind of ridicule captured by the phrase 'white men can't jump.' Since jumping is a skill that females are thought incapable of, there is the potential for a black male parodying a white male athlete to 'effeminize' this performance.
36 Butler, *Bodies That Matter*, 129

37 Ibid.

38 Parody by athletic women of other athletic women might expose the racialization of femininity. A white female athlete impersonating a black female athlete may attribute athletic skills, for example, jumping ability and exaggerated physical strength (and hence masculinity), to the black athlete that she might not attribute in the same measure to herself as a white athlete, thus underlining her own ambivalent relationship to the constitutive demands of both sport and femininity. An impersonation of a white female athlete by a black female athlete, by contrast, might attribute a 'femininity as incompetence' to the white athlete, thus distancing her from conventional (white) femininity and exposing a break in the presumed continuity between female sexed bodies and conventional femininity. For those who equate white femininity with femininity, this parody is likely to reconfigure popular cultural notions that, as a black woman, she is not 'really' feminine.

39 I am grateful to Kathleen Rockhill for this point from her presentation 'On the Matter of Bodies.'

40 An interesting empirical question is whether those athletes who contend with multiple conflicting disciplines are more likely to actively resist sport discipline.

41 In order for there to be multiple possibilities for disruption to sport discipline, hybrid athletes cannot be hybrids in the same way. Even though interests from outside sport disrupt the demands of high-performance sport, disruption is less effective if everyone shares interests in sport, family, community, and nation. A sport ethics that encourages proliferation of diversity will be wary of attempts to distinguish the 'good' hybrid from the bad 'hybrid.' Representations in the popular press of Tiger Woods as the 'good' hybrid and of Dennis Rodman as the 'bad' hybrid, for example, introduce another set of standards for athlete identity. Woods, the Asian black golfer, brings diversity to a sport that has been predominately white, but his hybridity does little to disrupt professional golf. Representations of Woods as responsible and successful make it possible for him to be accommodated within professional golf. The 'bad' hybrid, Dennis Rodman, by contrast, is barely accommodated within professional basketball because his hybridity disrupts masculinity and sensibilities about the skills of basketball. See Plaschke, 'One Small Step for Golf ...,' C8.

42 König, 'Criticism of Doping,' 256

References

Adams, Mary Louise. 1995. 'Real Men Don't Wear Sequins: Sex, Gender and Figure Skating.' Presented to the Canadian Lesbian and Gay Studies Association. Montreal, 3 June.

Andrews, David L. 1993. 'Desperately Seeking Michel: Foucault's Genealogy, the Body, and Critical Sport Sociology.' *Sociology of Sport Journal* 10: 148–67.

– 1996. 'The Facts of Michael Jordan's Blackness: Excavating a Floating Racial Signifier.' *Sociology of Sport Journal* 13: 125–58.

Baier, Annette. 1988. 'Trust and Antitrust.' *Ethics* 96: 231–60.

Bale, John. 1994. *Landscapes of Modern Sport.* Leicester: Leicester University Press.

Barber, Benjamin. 1984. *Strong Democracy.* Berkeley: University of California Press.

Bartky, Sandra. 1990. 'Foucault, Femininity, and the Modernization of Patriarchal Power.' In S. Bartky, ed., *Femininity and Domination: Studies in the Phenomenology of Oppression,* 63–82. New York and London: Routledge.

Bauman, Zygmunt. 1992. *Intimations of Postmodernity.* London: Routledge.

Begley, Sharon. 1995. 'Three Is Not Enough: Surprising New Lessons from the Controversial Science of Race.' *Newsweek,* 13 Feb.: 67–9.

Berger, John. 1991. 'The Suit and the Photograph.' In Chandra Muerji and Michael Schudson, eds, *Rethinking Popular Culture: Contemporary Perspectives in Cultural Studies,* 424–31. Berkeley: University of California Press.

Bernauer, J.W. 1992. 'Beyond Life and Death: On Foucault's Post-Auschwitz Ethic.' In *Michel Foucault Philosopher,* 260–78. Trans. T.J. Armstrong. New York: Routledge.

Birrell, Susan. 1989. 'Racial Relations Theories and Sport: Suggestions for a More Critical Analysis.' *Sociology of Sport Journal* 6: 212–27.

Bleier, Ruth. 1984. *Science and Gender: A Critique of Biology and Its Theories on Women.* New York: Pergamon Press.

Bordo, Susan. 1990. 'Reading the Slender Body.' In M. Jacobus, E. Fox Keller, and

S. Shuttleworth, eds, *Body/Politics: Women and the Discourses of Science*, 83–112. New York and London: Routledge.

– 1991. 'Docile Bodies, Rebellious Bodies: Foucauldian Perspectives on Female Psychopathology.' In H.J. Silverman, ed., *Writing the Politics of Difference*, 203–15. Albany: State University of New York Press.

– 1992. 'Postmodern Subjects, Postmodern Bodies.' *Feminist Studies* 18(2): 159–75.

Brown, William. 1980. 'Ethics, Drugs, and Sport.' *Journal of the Philosophy of Sport* 7: 15–23.

– 1984. 'Paternalism, Drugs, and the Nature of Sports.' *Journal of the Philosophy of Sport* 11: 14–22.

Brownworth, Victoria. 1994. 'The Competitive Closet.' In Susan Fox Rogers, ed., *Sportsdykes*, 75–86. New York: St Martin's Press.

Burke, Phyllis. 1996. *Gender Shock: Exploding the Myths of Male & Female*. New York: Anchor Books.

Butler, Judith. 1986. 'Sex and Gender in Simone de Beauvoir's *Second Sex*.' In Helene Vivienne Wenzel, ed., *Simone de Beauvoir: Witness to a Century. Yale French Studies* 72: 35–49.

– 1990. *Gender Trouble: Feminism and the Subversion of Identity*. New York and London: Routledge.

– 1991. 'Imitation and Gender Subordination.' In Dianna Fuss, ed., *Inside/Out: Lesbian Theories, Gay Theories*, 13–31. New York and London: Routledge.

– 1992. 'Contingent Foundations: Feminism and the Question of "Postmodernism."' In J. Butler and J. Scott, eds, *Feminists Theorize the Political*, 3–22. New York and London: Routledge.

– 1993. *Bodies That Matter: On the Discursive Limits of 'Sex.'* New York and London: Routledge.

– 1993. 'Critically Queer.' *GLQ: A Journal of Lesbian and Gay Studies* 1(1): 17–32.

Cahn, Susan K. 1994. *Coming On Strong: Gender and Sexuality in Twentieth-Century Women's Sport*. Cambridge: Harvard University Press.

Canadian Centre for Drug-Free Sport. n.d. *Guide to Drug Free Sport*. Gloucester, ON: Canadian Centre for Drug-Free Sport.

Carron, A.V. 1984. 'Cohesion in Sport Teams.' In J.M. Silba and R. Weinberg, eds, *Psychological Foundations of Sport*, 340–51. Champaign, IL: Human Kinetics Publishers, Inc.

Chang, E.K. 1994. 'A Not-So-New Spelling of My Name: Notes Toward (and Against) a Politics of Equivocation.' In A. Bammer, ed., *Displacements: Cultural Identities in Question*, 251–66. Bloomington: Indiana University Press.

Christie, James. 1996. 'Basketball's Purist Bares All.' *Globe and Mail*, 8 May: C3.

Coaching Association of Canada. 1989. *National Coaching Certification Program (NCCP) Theory II.* Gloucester, ON: CAC.

– 1993. *National Coaching Certification Program (NCCP) Theory I.* Rev. ed. Gloucester, ON: CAC.

Coakley, Jay. 1994. *Sport in Society: Issues and Controversies.* St Louis: Mosby.

Cole, Cam. 1996. 'Men Making Moves in a New Arena.' Edmonton *Journal,* 14 Feb.: A1, A12.

Cole, Cheryl. 1993. 'Resisting the Canon: Feminist Cultural Studies, Sport, and Technologies of the Body.' *Journal of Sport and Social Issues* 17(2): 77–97.

Connell, R.W. 1983. *Which Way Is Up?: Essays on Class, Sex and Culture.* Sydney: George Allen & Unwin.

– 1990. 'An Iron Man: The Body and Some Contradictions of Hegemonic Masculinity.' In M.A. Messner and D.F. Sabo, eds, *Sport, Men, and the Gender Order: Critical Feminist Perspectives,* 83–95. Champaign, IL: Human Kinetics Books.

Cornell, Drucilla. 1992. *The Philosophy of the Limit.* New York and London: Routledge.

Costa, D.M., and S.R. Guthrie, eds. 1994. *Women and Sport: Interdisciplinary Perspectives.* Champaign, IL: Human Kinetics.

Creedon, Pamela J., ed. 1994. *Women, Media and Sport: Challenging Gender Values.* Thousand Oaks, CA: Sage Publications.

Cronon, W., ed. 1995. *Uncommon Ground: Toward Reinventing Nature.* New York and London: W.W. Norton and Co.

Daniels, Dayna. 1992. 'Gender (Body) Verification (Building).' *Play & Culture* 5: 370–7.

Davies, C., and A. Lonsbrough. 1995. 'Lost Chance to Halt the Rapist Coach.' *Daily Telegraph,* 28 Sept.: 3.

Davis, Laurel. 1990. 'The Articulation of Difference: White Preoccupation with the Question of Racially Linked Genetic Differences among Athletes.' *Sociology of Sport Journal* 7: 179–87.

Davis, Laurel, and Linda Delano. 1992. 'Fixing the Boundaries of Physical Gender: Side Effects of Anti-Drug Campaigns in Athletics.' *Sociology of Sport Journal* 9: 1–19.

Davis, Lennard J. 1995. *Enforcing Normalcy: Disability, Deafness and the Body.* London and New York: Versa.

Davis, R. 1994. 'Issues Related to Classification: Investigation Before Implementation.' In B. Steadward, E. Nelson, and G. Wheeler, eds, *Vista '93 – The Outlook: The Proceedings from Vista '93. An International Conference on High Performance Sport for Athletes with Disabilities,* 269–79. Edmonton: Rick Hansen Centre.

Dean, Mitchell. 1994. *Critical and Effective Histories: Foucault's Methods and Historical Sociology.* London and New York: Routledge.

Depauw, Karen P., and Susan J. Gavron. 1995. *Disability and Sport.* Champaign, IL: Human Kinetics.

Deveaux, Monique. 1994. 'Feminism and Empowerment: A Critical Reading of Foucault.' *Feminist Studies* 20(2): 223–47.

Dreyfus, H.L., and P. Rabinow. 1983. *Michel Foucault: Beyond Structuralism and Hermeneutics.* Chicago: University of Chicago Press.

Dubin, C.L. 1990. *Commission of Inquiry into the Use of Drugs and Banned Practices Intended to Increase Athletic Performance.* Ottawa, ON: Supply and Services Canada.

Duncan, Margaret C. 1994. 'The Politics of Women's Body Images and Practices: Foucault, The Panopticon, and Shape Magazine.' *Journal of Sport and Social Issues* 18(1): 48–65.

Dunn, J.M. 1997. *Special Physical Education: Adapted, Individualized, Developmental.* 7th ed. Madison, WI: Brown & Benchmark.

Edmonton *Journal.* 1996. 'Taking It to the Limit.' 9 May D6.

Fanon, F. 1967. *Black Skin White Masks.* New York: Grove Weidenfeld.

Fausto-Sterling, Anne. 1992. *Myths of Gender.* New York: Basic Books.

Filax, Gloria. 1997. 'Critical Pedagogy and Resistance: Resisting the Resistors.' *Journal of Educational Thought* 31(3): 259–69.

Fiske, John. 1993. 'Bodies of Knowledge.' *Power Plays Power Works.* London, New York: Verso.

Flax, Jane. 1992. 'The End of Innocence.' In Judith Butler and Joan Scott, eds, *Feminists Theorize the Political,* 445–63. New York and London: Routledge.

Ford, Maureen. 1989. 'Distrusting Gender.' Unpublished paper.

Foucault, Michel. 1972. *The Archaeology of Knowledge and the Discourse on Language.* New York: Pantheon Books.

– 1979. *Discipline and Punish: The Birth of the Prison.* Trans. A. Sheridan. New York: Vintage Books.

– 1980. *The History of Sexuality Volume I: An Introduction.* Trans. R. Hurley. New York: Vintage Books.

– 1980. 'Two Lectures.' In Colin Gordon, ed., *Power/Knowledge: Selected Interviews and Other Writings 1972–1977,* 78–108. New York: Pantheon Books.

– 1980. 'Truth and Power.' In Gordon, ed., *Power/Knowledge,* 109–33.

– 1980. 'Power and Strategies.' In Gordon, ed., *Power/Knowledge,* 134–45.

– 1983. 'The Subject and Power.' In H.L. Dreyfus and P. Rabinow, *Michel Foucault: Beyond Structuralism and Hermeneutics,* 208–26. Chicago: University of Chicago Press.

– 1984. 'What Is Enlightenment?' In P. Rabinow, ed., *The Foucault Reader,* 32–50.

– 1984. 'On the Genealogy of Ethics: An Overview of Work in Progress.' In Rabinow, ed., *The Foucault Reader,* 340–72. New York: Pantheon Books.

– 1984. 'Politics and Ethics: An Interview.' In Rabinow, ed., *The Foucault Reader*, 373–80.

– 1985. *The Use of Pleasure, Volume 2 of The History of Sexuality*. Trans. R. Hurley. New York: Vintage Books.

– 1986. *The Care of the Self: Volume 3 of The History of Sexuality*. Trans. R. Hurley. New York: Vintage Books.

– 1994. 'The Ethic of Care for the Self as a Practice of Freedom.' In James Bernauer and David Rasmussen, eds, *The Final Foucault*, 1–20. Cambridge, MA: MIT Press.

Fox, Edward, Richard Bowers, and Merele Foss. 1993. *The Physiological Basis for Exercise and Sport*. 5th ed. Madison, WI: WCB Brown and Benchmark Publishers.

Fraser, Nancy. 1989. *Unruly Practices: Power, Discourse, and Gender in Contemporary Social Theory*. Minneapolis: University of Minnesota Press.

Frye, Marilyn. 1983. *The Politics of Reality: Essays in Feminist Theory*. Trumansburg, NY: The Crossing Press.

– 1992. 'White Woman Feminist 1983–1992.' In *Willful Virgin: Essays in Feminism*, 147–69. Freedom, CA: The Crossing Press.

Galasso, P.J. 1988. 'Children in Organized Sport: Rights and Access to Justice.' In P.J. Galasso, ed., *Philosophy of Sport and Physical Activity: Issues and Concepts*, 319–23. Toronto: Canadian Scholars' Press.

Gilligan, Carol. 1982. *In a Different Voice: Psychological Theory and Women's Development*. Cambridge: Harvard University Press.

Giroux, Henry. 1994. *Disturbing Pleasures: Learning Popular Culture*. New York and London: Routledge.

Grimshaw, Jean. 1986. *Philosophy and Feminist Thinking*. Minneapolis: University of Minnesota Press.

Groce, N. 1985. *Everyone Here Spoke Sign Language*. Cambridge: Harvard University Press.

Hacking, Ian. 1987. 'Was There a Probabilistic Revolution, 1800–1930?' In M. Heidelberger, ed., *The Probabilistic Revolution: Vol. I, Ideas in History*, 45–55. Cambridge, MA: MIT Press.

– 1990. *The Taming of Chance*. Cambridge: Cambridge University Press.

Hall, Catherine. 1992. 'White Identities.' *New Left Review* (May/June): 114–19.

Haraway, Donna. 1991. 'A Cyborg Manifesto: Science, Technology, and Socialist Feminism in the Late Twentieth Century.' In *Simians, Cyborgs, and Women: The Reinvention of Nature*, 149–81. New York: Routledge.

Harding, Sandra. 1987. 'The Curious Coincidence of Feminine and African Moralities: Challenges for Feminist Theory.' In E. Feder Kittay and D.T. Meyers, eds, *Women and Moral Theory*, 296–315. Totowa, NJ: Rowman and Littlefield.

Hargreaves, Jennifer. 1994. *Sporting Females: Critical Issues in the History and Sociology of Women's Sports*. London and New York: Routledge.

Harvard Lampoon. 1975. *Women in Sports: Hit or Ms?* Boston.

Haug, Frigga, ed. 1987. *Female Sexualization*. London: Verso.

Heikkala, Juha. 1993. 'Discipline and Excel: Techniques of the Self and Body and the Logic of Competing.' *Sociology of Sport Journal* 10: 397–412.

Herrnstein, R., and C. Murray. 1994. *The Bell Curve: Intelligence and Class Structure in American Life*. New York: Free Press.

Hirst, Paul. 1974. *Knowledge and the Curriculum*. London: Routledge and Kegan Paul.

Hoberman, John. 1997. *Darwin's Athletes: How Sport Has Damaged Black America and Preserved the Myth of Race*. Boston: Houghton Mifflin Co.

Hood-Williams, John. 1995. 'Sexing the Athletes.' *Sociology of Sport Journal* 12: 290–305.

hooks, bell. 1992. 'Representing Whiteness in the Black Imagination.' In Lawrence Grossberg, Cary Nelson, and Paula Treichler, eds, *Cultural Studies*, 338–46. New York and London: Routledge.

– 1994. *Outlaw Culture: Resisting Representations*. New York and London: Routledge.

Houston, Barbara. 1989. 'Prolegomena to Future Caring.' In M.M. Brabeck, ed., *Who Cares?: Theory, Education, and Educational Implications of the Ethic of Care*, 84–100. New York: Praeger.

Hutcheon, Linda. 1989. *The Politics of Postmodernism*. London and New York: Routledge.

Jackson, R.W., and G.M. Davis. 1983. 'The Value of Sports and Recreation for the Physically Disabled.' *Orthopaedic Clinics of North America* 14(2): 301–15.

Kidd, Bruce. 1987. 'Sports and Masculinity.' In M. Kaufman, ed., *Beyond Patriarchy: Essays by Men on Pleasure, Power, and Change*, 250–65. Toronto and New York: Oxford University Press.

Kissling, Elizabeth. A. 1991. 'One Size Does Not Fit All, or How I Learned to Stop Dieting and Love the Body.' *Quest* 43: 135–47.

Kleinman, Seymour. 1979. 'The Significance of Human Movement: A Phenomenological Approach.' In Ellen Gerber and William Morgan, eds, *Sport and the Body: A Philosophical Symposium*, 177–80. Philadelphia: Lea and Febiger.

König, Eugen. 1995. 'Criticism of Doping: The Nihilistic Side of Technological Sport and the Antiquated View of Sport Ethics.' *International Review for the Sociology of Sport* 30(3/4): 247–61.

Kreighbaum, E., and K. Barthels. 1996. *Biomechanics: A Qualitative Approach for Studying Human Movement*. Boston: Allyn and Bacon.

Landers, Ann. 1996. Column in *Edmonton Journal*, 19 Nov.: C6.

Larson, C.E., and F.M.J. LaFasto. 1989. *TeamWork: What Must Go Right / What Can Go Wrong.* Newbury Park, CA: Sage Publications.

Leibovitz, Anne. 1996. 'An Olympic Portfolio.' Photographs in *Vanity Fair,* May (no. 429): 125–59.

Lenskyj, Helen. 1986. *Out of Bounds: Women, Sport and Sexuality.* Toronto: The Women's Press.

– 1994. 'Sexuality and Femininity in Sport Contexts: Issues and Alternatives.' *Sport and Social Issues* 18(4): 356–76.

Lindstrom, Hans. 1986. 'Sports Classification for Locomotor Disabilities: Integrated Versus Diagnostic Systems.' In Claudine Sherril, ed., *Sport and Disabled Athletes: The 1984 Olympic Scientific Congress Proceedings,* 131–6. Champaign, IL: Human Kinetics Publishers, Inc.

Lugones, Maria. 1987. 'Playfulness, "World"-Travelling, and Loving Perception.' *Hypatia: A Journal of Feminist Philosophy* 2(2): 3–20.

Lyon, David. 1994. *Postmodernity.* Minneapolis: University of Minnesota Press.

Mackenzie, D.A. 1981. *Statistics in Britain 1865–1930: The Social Construction of Scientific Knowledge.* Edinburgh: Edinburgh University Press.

Magill, R.A. 1993. *Motor Learning: Concepts and Applications.* 4th ed. Madison, WI: WCB Brown and Benchmark.

Majors, Richard. 1990. 'Cool Pose: Black Masculinity and Sports.' In D. Messner and D. Sabo, eds, *Sport, Men, and the Gender Order: Critical Feminist Perspectives,* 109–14. Champaign, IL: Human Kinetics Books.

Marshall, James. 1989. 'Foucault and Education.' *Australia Journal of Education* 33(2): 99–113.

Martindale, Kathleen. 1992. 'Theorizing Autobiography and Materialist Feminist Pedagogy.' *Canadian Journal of Education* 17(3): 321–34.

May, T. 1993. *Between Genealogy and Epistemology: Psychology, Politics, and Knowledge in the Thought of Michel Foucault.* University Park: Pennsylvania State University Press.

McCarten, James. 1997. 'Report of Sexual Abuse Shatters Hockey World.' *Edmonton Journal,* 7 Jan.: D3.

McDermott, R., and H. Varenne. 1995. 'Culture *as* Disability.' *Anthropology and Education Quarterly* 26(3): 324–48.

McKay, Jim, Jennifer Gore, and David Kirk. 1990. 'Beyond the Limits of Technocratic Physical Education.' *Quest* 42(1): 52–76.

McNay. Lois. 1992. *Foucault and Feminism.* Boston: Northeastern University Press.

Messner, Michael A. 1992. *Power at Play: Sports and the Problem of Masculinity.* Boston: Beacon Press.

– 1994. 'Ah, Ya Throw Like a Girl!' In M.A. Messner and D.F. Sabo, eds, *Sex, Violence & Power in Sports,* 28–32. Freedom, CA: The Crossing Press.

- 1994. 'Gay Athletes and the Gay Games: An Interview with Tom Waddell.' In Messner and Sabo, eds, *Sex, Violence & Power in Sports*, 113–19.

Messner, Michael A., and Don F. Sabo. 1994. *Sex, Violence & Power in Sports*. Freedom, CA: The Crossing Press.

Miller, James. 1993. *The Passion of Michel Foucault*. New York: Anchor Books.

Minson, Jeffrey. 1985. *Genealogy of Morals: Nietzsche, Foucault, Donzelot and the Eccentricity of Ethics*. London: Macmillan.

Montgomery, Sue. 1996. 'Iron Ladies: Transvestite Team Wraps Up Thai Volleyball.' *The New Internationalist* 285 (Nov.): 6.

Moore, M.C. 1987. 'Ethical Discourse and Foucault's Conception of Ethics.' *Human Studies* 10: 81–95.

Morgan, Kathryn. 1991. 'Women and the Knife: Cosmetic Surgery and the Colonization of Women's Bodies.' *Hypatia: A Journal of Feminist Philosophy* 6(3): 23–53.

Murdoch, Iris. 1970. *The Sovereignty of Good*. London: Routledge and Kegan Paul.

Naylor, J. 1995. 'Growing Up – And Throwing Up – In Elite Sports.' *Globe and Mail*, 10 June: C24, C21.

Newsweek. 1995. 'What Colour Is Black?: Science, Politics, and Racial Identity.' 13 Feb.

Nickson, Liz. 1996. 'She's Not Heavy, She's My Sister.' *Globe and Mail*, 13 April: D3.

Nideffer, Robert. 1980. 'Attentional Focus – Self Assessment.' In R. Suinn, ed., *Psychology in Sports: Methods and Applications*, 281–90. Minneapolis, MN: Burgess Pub. Co.

Oliver, M. 1996. *Understanding Disability: From Theory to Practice*. London: Macmillan.

Painter, N.R. 1992. 'Hill, Thomas, and the Use of Racial Stereotype.' In Toni Morrison, ed., *Race-ing Justice, En-gendering Power: Essays on Anita Hill, Clarence Thomas, and the Construction of Social Reality*, 200–14. New York: Pantheon Books.

Pearson, Kathleen. 1979. 'Deception, Sportsmanship and Ethics.' In Ellen Gerber and William Morgan, eds, *Sport and the Body: A Philosophical Symposium*, 272–3. Philadelphia: Lea and Febiger.

Plaschke, Bill. 1997. 'One Small Step for Golf ...' *Edmonton Journal*, 21 May: C6.

Polanyi, Michael. 1964. *Personal Knowledge*. New York: Harper Torchbooks.

Porter, T.M. 1986. *The Rise of Statistical Thinking 1820–1900*. Princeton: Princeton University Press.

Pronger, Brian. 1990. 'Gay Jocks: A Phenomenology of Gay Men in Athletics.' In D. Messner and D. Sabo, eds, *Sport, Men, and the Gender Order: Critical Feminist Perspectives*, 141–52. Champaign, IL: Human Kinetics Books.

- 1992. *The Arena of Masculinity: Sports, Homosexualiy, and the Meaning of Sex*. Toronto: University of Toronto Press.

Rail, Genevieve, and Jean Harvey. 1995. 'Body at Work: Michel Foucault and the Sociology of Sport.' *Sociology of Sport Journal* 12: 164–79.

Rajchman, J. 1992. 'Foucault: The Ethic and The Work.' In *Michel Foucault Philosopher*, 215–22. Trans. T.J. Armstrong. New York: Routledge.

Ravizza, K., and K. Daruty. 1984. 'Paternalism and Sovereignty in Athletics: Limits and Justifications of the Coach's Exercise of Authority over the Adult Athlete.' *Journal of the Philosophy of Sport* 11: 71–82.

Real, Michael R. 1996. 'The Postmodern Olympics: Technology and the Commodification of the Olympic Movement.' *Quest* 49: 9–24.

Rees, C. Roger. 1996. 'Race and Sport in Global Perspective: Lessons from Post-Apartheid South Africa.' *Journal of Sport and Social Issues* 20(1): 22–32.

Rockhill, Kathleen. 1996. 'On the Matter of Bodies: Thinking through Judith Butler's Theory of Performativity in Relation to Sexuality, Race, and Dis/ability.' Paper presented to the Canadian Lesbian and Gay Studies Association, Brock University, 2 June.

Rodman, Dennis. 1996. *Bad as I Wanna Be.* New York: Delacorte Press.

Roxxie. 1993. 'Hockey Action: Beehives!' *Girljock* 9: 14–15.

Sabo, Don. 1994. 'The Politics of Homophobia in Sport.' In Messner and Sabo, eds, *Sex, Violence & Power in Sports.* Freedom, CA: The Crossing Press.

Schellenberger, H. 1990. *Psychology of Team Sports.* Toronto: Sports Books Publishers.

Scott, J. 1992. '"Experience."' In J. Butler and J. Scott, eds, *Feminists Theorize the Political*, 22–40. New York and London: Routledge.

Sedgwick, Eve Kosofsky. 1993. *Tendencies.* Durham: Duke University Press.

Sherwin, Susan. 1992. *No Longer Patient: Feminist Ethics and Health Care.* Philadelphia: Temple University Press.

Shogan, Debra. 1978. 'Alberta's Combination Press.' *Scholastic Coach* 48(2): 64–5.

– 1980. 'And Now for the One Hand Chest Pass.' *Scholastic Coach* 50(3): 52, 54.

– 1981. Instructional Video. University of Alberta, Edmonton.

– 1982. 'Defending the Offside Screen.' *Athletic Journal* 62(10): 22–3.

– 1988. 'Inequality in Sport and the Logic of Gender.' In P.J. Galasso, ed., *Philosophy of Sport and Physical Activity: Issues and Concepts*, 271–6. Toronto: Canadian Scholars' Press.

– 1988. 'Rules, Penalties and Officials: Sport and the Legality-Morality Distinction.' In Galasso, ed., *Philosophy of Sport and Physical Activity*, 343–51.

– 1988. 'The Prisoner's Dilemma in Competitive Sport: Moral Decision-Making vs. Prudence.' In Galasso, ed., *Philosophy of Sport and Physical Activity*, 405–9.

– 1988. *Care and Moral Motivation.* Toronto: OISE Press.

– 1990. 'Comments on Hawkesworth's "Knowers, Knowing, Known": Feminist Theory and Claims of Truth.' *Signs: Journal of Women in Culture and Society* 15(2): 424–5.

- 1991. 'Trusting Paternalism? Trust as a Condition for Paternalistic Decisions.' *Journal of the Philosophy of Sport* 18(1): 49–58.
- 1993. 'Conceptualizing Agency: Implications for Feminist Ethics.' In *A Reader in Feminist Ethics*, 333–42. Toronto: Canadian Scholars' Press.
Shumway, D.R. 1989. *Michel Foucault.* Charlottesville: University Press of Virginia.
Suits, Bernard. 1978. *The Grasshopper: Games, Life and Utopia.* Toronto: University of Toronto Press.
Syer, John. 1986. *Team Spirit: The Elusive Experience.* London: Kingswood Press.
Thomas, Carolyn. 1988. 'Criteria for Athlete Autonomy in a Paternalistic Sport Model.' In S. Ross and L. Chaquette, eds, *Persons, Minds, and Bodies*, 191–202. North York, ON: University Press of Canada.
Thompson, P. 'Privacy and the Urinalysis Testing of Athletes.' *Journal of the Philosophy of Sport* 9: 60–5.
Tong, Rosemarie. 1993. *Feminine and Feminist Ethics.* Belmont, CA: Wadsworth Publishing Co.
Townley, Barbara. 1994. *Reframing Human Resource Management: Power, Ethics, and the Subject at Work.* Thousand Oaks, CA: Sage Publications.
United Nations. 1983. *World Programme of Action Concerning Disabled Persons.* U.N. Decade of Disabled Persons 1983–1992. New York: United Nations.
Usher, Robin, and Richard Edwards. 1994. *Postmodernism and Education.* London and New York: Routledge.
Vanlandewijck, Y.C., and R.J. Chappel. 1996. 'Integration and Classification Issues in Competitive Sports for Athletes with Disabilities.' *Sport Science Review* 5(1): 65–88.
Vigarello, Georges. 1995. 'The Life of the Body in *Discipline and Punish*.' *Sociology of Sport Journal* 12: 158–63.
Warner, Michael. 1994. 'Introduction.' In Michael Warner, ed., *Fear of a Queer Planet*, vii–xxxi. Minneapolis: University of Minnesota Press.
Warren, W.E., and L.F. Chapman. 1992. *Basketball Coach's Survival Guide: Practical Techniques and Materials for Building an Effective Program and a Winning Team.* West Nyack, NY: Parker Publishing Co.
Weedon, Chris. 1987. *Feminist Practice and Poststructuralist Theory.* Oxford: Basil Blackwell.
Wendell, Susan. 1989. 'Toward a Feminist Theory of Disability.' *Hypatia: A Journal of Feminist Philosophy* 4(2): 104–24.
Whitson, David. 1990. 'Sport in the Social Construction of Masculinity.' In M.A. Messner and D.F. Sabo, eds, *Sport, Men, and the Gender Order: Critical Feminist Perspectives*, 19–29. Champaign, IL: Human Kinetics Books.
- 1994. 'The Embodiment of Gender: Discipline, Domination, and Empower-

ment.' In S. Birrell and C. Cole, eds, *Women, Sport, and Culture,* 353–72. Champaign, IL: Human Kinetics Press.

Williams, Patricia. 1995. *The Rooster's Egg: On the Persistence of Prejudice.* Cambridge: Harvard University Press.

Willis, P. 1977. *Learning to Labour: How Working-Class Kids Get Working-Class Jobs.* Farnborough, Eng.: Saxon House.

Young, Iris M. 1980. 'Throwing Like a Girl: A Phenomenology of Feminine Body Comportment, Motility and Spatiality.' *Human Studies* 3(137): 137–56.

Zeigler, Earle. 1988. 'Coach and Athlete – In Each Other's Power.' In P.J. Galasso, ed., *Philosophy of Sport and Physical Activity: Issues and Concepts,* 242–51. Toronto: Canadian Scholars' Press.

Index